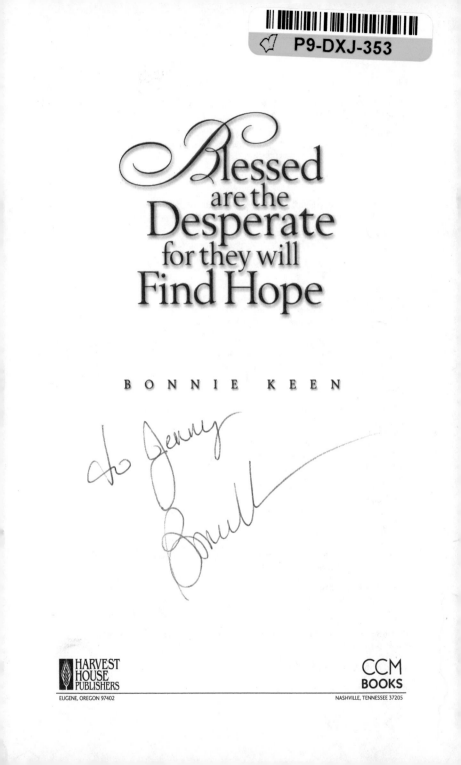

Blessed
are the
Desperate
for they will
Find Hope

BONNIE KEEN

To Jenny

Bonnie Keen

HARVEST
HOUSE
PUBLISHERS

EUGENE, OREGON 97402

CCM
BOOKS

NASHVILLE, TENNESSEE 37205

Bible version used in this book:

The Holy Bible, New Century Version, Copyright © 1987, 1988, 1991 by Word Publishing, Nashville, TN 37214. Used by permission.

The Amplified Bible, Old Testament, Copyright © 1965 and 1987 by The Zondervan Corporation, and from The Amplified New Testament, Copyright © 1954, 1958, 1987 by The Lockman Foundation. Used by permission.

The Message. Copyright © 1993, 1994, 1995, 1996. Used by permission of NavPress Publishing Group.

The Living Bible, Copyright © 1971 owned by assignment by Illinois Regional Bank N.A. (as trustee). Used by permission of Tyndale House Publishers, Inc., Wheaton, Illinois 60189. All rights reserved.

The King James Version of the Bible.

Cover by PAZ Design Group, Salem, Oregon

The Scripture quotation on pages 67,68 is Romans 8:38,39 AMP.
The Scripture quotation on page 72 is Proverbs 16:3 TLB.
The Scripture quotation on page 117 is John 20:23 AMP.
The Scripture quotation on page 161 is Isaiah 54:4-7 NCV.

The song quotation on pages 98,99 is from "Let the Healing Begin" by Lowell Alexander and Cheryl Rogers: © Copyright 1995 Bridge Building Music, Inc. / Molto Bravo! Music, Inc. (BMI) (all rights administered by Brentwood-Benson Music Publishing, Inc.) / Word Music (ASCAP). All rights reserved. Used by permission; *and* © Copyright 1995 Cheryl Rogers. Used by permission.

BLESSED ARE THE DESPERATE FOR THEY WILL FIND HOPE
Text Copyright © 2000 by Bonnie Keen
Published by Harvest House Publishers
Eugene, Oregon 97402 and
CCM Books, a Division of CCM Communications
Nashville, Tennessee 37205

Library of Congress Cataloging-in-Publication Data
Keen, Bonnie, 1955-
    Blessed are the desperate for they will find hope / Bonnie Keen.
        p. cm.
    ISBN 0-7369-0242-2
    1. Keen, Bonnie, 1955- 2. Christian biography—United States. 3. Divorced
    mothers—United States—Biography. 4. Women musicians—United States—Biography.
    5. First Call (Musical group) I. Title.

BR1725.K39 A3 2000
277.3'0825'092—dc21
[B]   00-033485

Printed in the United States of America.

00 01 02 03 04 05 06 07 08 09 / BP-MS / 10 9 8 7 6 5 4 3 2 1

To my miracles,
Brent, Courtney, and Graham...

"You're blessed when you're at the end of your rope. With less of you there is more of God and his rule. You're blessed when you feel you've lost what is most dear to you. Only then can you be embraced by the One most dear to you."

—Matthew 5:3,4 THE MESSAGE

Embrace the day and hold it near
It will not pass this way again
Then maybe we'll discover
A miracle uncovered
When the now begins

—Bonnie Keen and Lowell Alexander, from "When the Now Begins"

CONTENTS

Prelude: I Believe You

One: COLORS
God and the Wizard of Oz 18
Alice 23
The Preacher 28
Fierce Intentions 30
Keeping the Monsters at Bay 35

Two: RED
Numb 49
Broken Places 53
Bridges 57
Drop of Red 64
Broken Bones 66

Three: ORANGE
The Fine Art of Fighting 74
Hope 80
Conversation with the Devil 87
Desperate for God 94
Let the Healing Begin 98

Four: YELLOW
Bridge Child 106
Suffering 110
What We Know 113
Foot Washing 115
Sisters 119

Five: GREEN

Crazy Grace 133

Chariots of Fire 138

Traditions Redeemed 143

Rock Flowers 150

Six: BLUE

Bringing Up Eve 157

Insanity 163

Understanding 166

Finish Second 173

Seven: PURPLE

Just One More 183

Something to Hold On To 185

Trust God and Enjoy the Kiwi 189

Baptism 192

Blessed Are the Desperate 195

Eight: RAINBOW

Holy Ground 198

Epilogue

My Hall of Famers

I Believe You

~

Believe me—many times over the course of working on this book, I've asked myself what is driving me to pull out my personal journals and write down some of the most personal, private, painful moments of my past and have them published. Could it be that narcissism, pride, or insanity has moved me to this?

I've journaled almost every day of my life, but that's been my own medicine, my own therapy, my own way of sorting through the events in my world. As a child not permitted to show anger, I used my diary to vent my rage. I'd take a pen or crayon and just dig into the paper with huge slashes and marks and maybe one little sentiment, like "I'm so mad!!!" I needed a safe place to let out my deepest surges of fears, rage, questions, and prayers, and my diary never turned away. Likewise, my journal has always been there, ready to be attacked or overused, but always willing to hear what I have to say.

During my recovery from an episode of clinical depression in 1995, I remember feeling the presence of God—it felt sort of like He was watching over my shoulder—as I went through my daily ritual of scrawling in my beloved journal. When I got to the ugliest parts (some of which were about Him: why in the world He wasn't bringing some relief to my life, skepticism that He really was able to do all things in His time—the sort of stuff you wouldn't exactly want God to actually see), I assumed He'd be disgusted enough to back away and leave me to my heretical ranting.

But quite the opposite thing happened. It seemed like the great Author of the sky was saying, "This is good. Write it all down. Just keep writing."

I asked Him point-blank, "Why do You care? Have You seen this part about how I would really like to go ahead and have You take me out, except that I know my kids would suffer? Have you seen this 'I want to die' part?"

But God seemed not the least bit rattled by this, and with His hand on my shoulder—or at times a heel of the Almighty's foot in the small of my back—I continued to sense His calm encouragement. "Just keep writing," He repeated.

And so here it is: "Blessed are the desperate for they will find hope." The hope thing didn't happen for a while. But as my desperation continued to move me closer to God, closer to touching the hem of Christ's garment, closer to His cross, I clung to Him with all I had. My circumstances didn't change...but my heart did. He allowed me to lie down in green pastures, and He led me to still waters.

In 1995, I sang at a singles' event in Detroit during a Valentine's Day conference. I was terrified to share about my own divorce—the fears and failure I felt as a single mom of two kids, a woman now in depression. I was afraid if anyone saw what a basket case I was, they'd pick up the nearest hymnal and cry out, "Stone her!"

While I spoke, I kept crunching and uncrunching the jotted-over piece of my journal I held in my pocket. Then something happened that day to cause me to take it out. It was Valentine's Day, and I was lonely as usual, fighting the anger I felt as I remembered the cutesy little commercials I'd seen about giving diamonds to that glorious woman in your life...or the Godiva chocolate specials all wrapped up in glowing splendor at the mall...or Hallmark's mushy-gushy love cards at every grocery store. Once again, the whole world was in love—everyone but me!

Halfway through the concert, I looked out at the sea of faces sitting there and suddenly I knew I was in a room full of comrades. These people were at a singles' event on Valentine's weekend...*alone*. It was like an AA meeting for believers struggling with romance. "Hi, I'm Bonnie," I wanted to say, "and I'm addicted to believing there just might be another chance for me to love again...someday...if God would just look this way and notice me screaming about it!"

That day in Detroit, I nervously launched into the private, vulnerable underbelly of my life. These poor, unsuspecting people were given, in a nutshell, the description of my wretched heart. We laughed about some things, and then I pulled out the journal segment and read it aloud. By the time I'd finished, I was crying, the audience was standing and crying, and I knew why God had been telling me to keep writing everything down.

The piece I read went something like this: "What would I say to someone in this valley? I'd say hold on to what you know to be true about God's faithfulness. Try not to buy into what you see around you. Fight hard against the darkness—but once you've reached the end of your fighting, let go and embrace the despair. Let go and fall apart. God will hold you up and surprise you with His unending mercy. This collapse, what feels like the end of your life, is actually the first chapter in the beginning. From Eden until now, you have been marked for *life*."

Some time later, I recorded a companion project for this book called *Marked for Life* and was meeting about *Blessed Are the Desperate* with the staff of my publishing house. After the meeting was over, one of the company executives lingered. She hadn't said much during the meeting, as I'd been speaking at high speed and with great passion and enthusiasm about my hopes and prayers for this book. But this woman touched my arm and put into three simple words what I'd spent 30 minutes trying to articulate. "It seems to me," she said, "you just want to say to others, 'I believe you.'"

Yes. That's why I lifted the shirt of my life to show my scars and then how God healed me and continues to heal me. I want to shout this as loudly as I can to anyone who sits in the seat I know so well:

I believe you!

I believe you when you say you love God and still doubt Him because of the pain in your soul.

I believe you when you say you're afraid to let anyone know how badly you hurt, especially at church, for fear of rejection.

I believe you when you say you are blindsided by losing your job and you have a family to feed.

I believe you when you say you long for love, for a spouse, for a first, second, or third chance to be the man or woman God created you to be, in a godly relationship. But you feel unworthy...and the years go by....

I believe you when you say you ache from the betrayal of a spouse, a friend, a colleague at work, a parent....

I believe you when you say that the black hole, what William Styron calls "the visible darkness," threatens to pull you under in a tide that makes you long for death.

I believe you when you say you fear that Christ died on that cross for everyone but you and your circumstances.

I believe you when you say you see the umbrella of God's grace extended and you can't find a way to see yourself under its covering.

I believe your doubts.

I believe your pain.

I believe your fears even though, as a person of faith, you are horribly ashamed to have such doubts, pain, or fear.

And the reason I want to say "I believe you" is because I've tasted those bitter waters. You are not alone. I believe, too, that what God did with my desperation, I *know* He longs to do for you.

God believes you and He hears every breath of your prayers.

Christ died for every season of hopelessness, fear, doubt, pain, loss, hurt, betrayal, and failure. He was a man of sorrows, acquainted with grief. He was homeless, loved by few, betrayed, and despised.

Christ, the heart of the Father, spent His life showing us the nature of God. On earth, He hung out with people like us. The desperate ones. We are the ones who crack open and are most likely to let Him in.

There is no end to His mercy.

There is no length He will not go to—to hold you up, to bring you back, and to deliver you to a new life.

His timing is perfect. Trust Him with your dreams.

Your circumstances do not define you. They try to beat you up one side and down the other and convince you that all is lost. Let your heart see beyond them into what only God knows waits for you.

The cross of Christ stands to stare down defeat. All can never be lost again because of Him.

I believe you because I've been there and seen what God can do with messy lives.

So I pray that the muck and mire, the hopes and dreams realized in this scrapbook of my life, will say to you what I know. In the face of Christ, we see the face of a human and the face of our humanity. Through our stories, we find each other's stories, and I hope that something in this book will speak to a piece of your life that, like mine, resonates with pain. And I hope that something in this book will allow you to savor the precious aftertaste of grace.

I have lived the timeworn expressions I write here, and now they are like a covering over my heart—I know that nothing can separate us from the love of God in Christ. And that in time, all things do work together for good for those of us who can hold on and love Him even if it means we just *want to love* Him. He patiently waits for us to let Him hold us and comfort us and move us on. Jesus loves me this I know—because His Word tells me so. The world and the conditions we find ourselves in are lies. The Word of God is our only truth.

Nothing is wasted.

Believe me.

One
COLORS

Two
RED

Three
ORANGE

Four
YELLOW

Five
GREEN

Six
BLUE

Seven
PURPLE

Eight
RAINBOW

"It is not as a boy that I confess Christ, but my Hosanna has passed through a great furnace of doubt."

—Fyodor Dostoyevsky, *The Brothers Karamazov*

December, 1989

I saw an interesting picture of my great-grandmother today. She was 18 years of age, standing staring straight into the camera, with one hand on her waist and flaming red hair that fell just as far. The family said, "She looks like a witch!" but I am struck by her strength and air of spirit. She was the baby, brought over from Ireland in her mother's arms when her mother went to say "good-bye" to her father and the boat taking him to America took off with her in it.

Lyric idea for the women I admire and the ones who've come before:

> "You have the heart of a fighter in your
> fragile frame
> The red blood of courage is running through
> your veins
> You've made an art of surviving in the
> middle of your pain
> By holding on to what you believe."

June, 1990

David, my counselor, told me today that as he listens to me talk, I seem to be living somewhere between the Old and New Testaments—with little sense of mercy or forgiveness.

1993

Called mom's house tonight from the road. Courtney answered and I am flooded with gratitude, as she and Graham sounded cheerful and happy. They were making cookies at their grandmother's house! What a blessing to have my precious parents in their lives. So very much, I want my kids to make it through this wiser than I have been.

1996

I know I'm breaking a generational pattern with the women in my family by going through my divorce. I continue to ask God in His mercy to walk me as His daughter through this with dignity and humility...and that somehow this experience will be spared my own children and used for His glory.

1997

Give us this day, our daily bread....Give me this day, as a woman who wants to do the next right thing, just enough daily manna of grace to walk on....

God and the Wizard of Oz

~

"This is what the LORD says, who made you,
who formed you in your mother's body, who will help you...
I will pour out water for the thirsty land and make
streams flow on dry land. I will pour out my Spirit into your
children and my blessing on your descendants."

—ISAIAH 44:2,3 NCV

As a child, my main battles seemed to be for things like being able to watch the annual television broadcast of *The Wizard of Oz*, which always aired on Sunday nights. But Sunday nights were dedicated to church.

Being in church three times a week, whether I needed it or not, must have given me some major brownie points in the heavenly records. At least I hoped it would. Because it was painful, sometimes, to miss out on life by having to sit in a pew in church. At least I *felt* like I was missing the best parts of life. Like *The Wizard of Oz*.

When I was young, I missed *The Wizard of Oz* for years. We had to be in church every Sunday night, and we always left the house just when the black and white turned to magical colors as Dorothy opened her door in Oz to find the Munchkins and the Yellow Brick Road. Good grief! Wasn't life in Christ about changing our dull lives to something vivid and real and alive? Couldn't I spend just one stinking Sunday night at home watching this unbelievable movie? Would I go flaming into oblivion if I wasn't sitting in the eighth row down on the right aisle with my parents for one Sunday night of the year?

When I look back, it's almost funny to think of how much I longed to see this movie. Yet this longing doesn't seem so funny when I realize that it also seems to represent the overall struggle I had with God—how He said He longed for me to know life in all its abundance, but I seemed to be denied the abundant part.

I was a straight-A student in school who lived in mortal fear of doing anything wrong. I remember one time in the third grade when I lied to my teacher about where I'd hung my coat in the cloakroom. I went home, mortified, and wrote God a letter begging Him to forgive me and not to send me to hell for telling this first deliberate lie of my life.

God was scary. God did not want anyone to enjoy anything. God did not like *The Wizard of Oz*. If one wanted to watch incredible, thrilling musicals, one would just have to wait for a time when maybe God's back was turned. Or when a blizzard hit uncharacteristically in the middle of summer so everyone would be forced to stay home and see the Emerald City and glittery slippers!

I also figured that God must not like music. Well, maybe He liked Bach or musical events that happened by accident outside of church—but probably not. I loved music, craved it. On my bed in my room, I'd listen to musical theater albums, Rachmaninoff, Barbra Streisand, Steppenwolf. Was I wicked? Was I nuts?

By the time I'd accepted that Oz just wasn't my future, I began to believe that I would have to pursue the arts in spite of God's wrath and fury and timetables for proper Sunday night activities.

Quietly, secretly, I immersed myself in music, studying the harmony of Three Dog Night, The Fifth Dimension, and

Sondheim musicals, never aware that the Second Chapter of Acts was waiting at my local Christian bookstore. I hoped God wouldn't be on duty when I did the musical revues and plays that so filled my soul with life and fulfillment. Why did He give me these gifts? How was I supposed to find a place for myself?

Now, all denominations and religious institutions have their own special idiosyncrasies. And it never ceases to amaze me to what lengths we humans will go to try to rewrite or make more complicated the simple story of the gospel. We add little rules and regulations, most of which are self-imposed, well-meant but legalistic in nature. The church of my youth was no exception.

One of the top ten "no-no's" in my church was using instrumental music in the actual church service. I was taught that any use of instrumentation or choral singing or, worse yet, solo singing would send one straight to Hades. We were taught that the verse in Ephesians that read, "Sing and make melody in your hearts to the Lord," meant we could only make a melody if we all made it together—no organ, no piano, no choir, just an a cappella gang hymn-singing thing.

Growing up as a person God had gifted to sing and play piano and write and act and, yes, even dance, what was I to do? Ever since I'd been born in September of 1955, my mom had been convinced that God in His infinite wisdom had dropped a child prodigy into her southern, white, middle-class suburban world. At age three, I sealed my fate by hearing a melody of some sort on television and playing it back by ear on my little almost-piano. That was all it took for mom. "For unto her a star was born," she seemed to claim.

For the next 13 years mom dragged me to auditions, had me playing the piano for the milkman and mailman—bringing them into the house to hear me play whether they wanted to or not—for the relatives, for anyone she could find. The precious part is how she encouraged me, drove me countless miles, and paid hundreds of dollars in order to cultivate in me what she interpreted as pure talent. She believed in me and gave me courage when I didn't have any of my own. And I began down a path that she had always dreamed of for herself but was never given the opportunity to follow. Having a mom who believed in every breath I took gave me a sense of abandon and a willingness to do the ridiculous. It also sometimes made it overwhelmingly hard for me to live up to the expectations I felt. But I was just loony enough to do things like give myself the name Julie Rose because I didn't like my own name anymore. By age eight, I—or rather Julie Rose—was writing songs. When I started my own publishing company as an adult, I named it Julie Rose Music in honor of this imaginary other me.

Sweet daddy, quiet and gracious, allowed mom to leave him out of our artistic excursions. Silence and humility were not new to him. As a young man in the Army during the Korean War, he had been one in a very select group of men chosen to study the effects of the atomic bomb. This was top secret, and the FBI interviewed everyone from his kindergarten teacher on up to check him out. My daddy was a brilliant man, yet I never heard him speak of this part of his life until after I was first married, and even then he didn't say much about it until I squealed, "Dad, this is incredible! Why didn't you *tell* me about this before?" To which he grinned and shyly shrugged his shoulders.

As mom and I expanded my experiences with performance and music and acting and theater outside of the church arena, I remained unable to express myself artistically where it truly mattered—in my faith.

Over time, my feelings about churchgoing turned a corner. Now I understood why what I'd heard preached did not line up with my inside feelings and prayers. I discovered that Jesus, the Son of God, and the expression of who He was could never be boring! And I realized that God's love for me was not based wholly on my performance.

Performance. This became a word that integrated my faith with my gifting. I'd tried to keep the performances right on every front, and I knew that from time to time I would fall very short of what was expected. But the fear began to dissipate.

"Couldn't we miss just one service?" I'd ask when *The Wizard of Oz* was once again airing on Sunday night. "Couldn't I watch Dorothy's journey and learn lessons along the way about courage, wisdom, growing a heart, and rescuing Toto, too?"

"Of course not," they would say. "It's church night."

But God didn't leave me in the lurch.

In the early '80s, I received a call from my next-door neighbor, who managed a young recording artist named Amy. "Would you like to sing backup vocals on a short tour with a new girl we have, Amy Grant?"

"Sure!" I answered, thrilled to have work. I'd never been to a single Christian concert, and my first one was to be onstage, singing with a group of background vocalists behind Amy Grant, with DeGarmo and Key as her band. I remember crying with such release and joy at the discovery of how real this was. In fact, one of the managers asked me to hold it together a little more during the concert, as I was distracting with the Kleenex and all. I was amazed at how faith could be written and sung about in this way.

The beauty and magic of writing, singing, performing, and communicating about my passion, my Christ, and the wonder of this God who cannot be limited to nights of the week or a magician behind a curtain survived and grew in me over the years.

And here I have to admit something to you. As soon as I was able to, I went out and bought my very own Golden Edition, MGM Special Video copy of *The Wizard of Oz.* And yes, I have pulled it out for an occasional Sunday-night viewing.

Alice

~

At age 11, I fell hopelessly, permanently in love with the theater. For many years I had relentlessly tormented the kids in my neighborhood, coaxing them to be in all kinds of backyard productions—things like a reenactment from the vampire soap opera *Dark Shadows*, complete with mom's ketchup for blood.

I'd done two plays at my public elementary school, one of which I had written. It was called *Lonely Helena*, and all I remember about it was a huge pillow fight at the climax where Helena fights back against the girls who'd kept her under their thumb. Even as a child, I had strains of melodrama running through me.

As it happened, however, in the spring of 1967 the local government-funded children's theater, Nashville Academy Theater, held open auditions for its upcoming rendition of Lewis Carroll's *Alice in Wonderland*. In the newspaper a black-and-white drawing taken from Carroll's book was printed beside the details about the time and place of the auditions. It took my mom one look at the ad and then at my long blonde hair, blue eyes, and skinny frame to decide this was a potential lead role for me.

I had never been to a "big" audition before, and this one was a doozy. From the moment we stepped into the semi-dark, cool auditorium of the theater, I was entranced. The set for the current production was on the stage, and colorful lights shone down on the people milling about carrying important-looking clipboards and obviously somehow connected with the whole thing. It took me a moment to realize that the room was filled with a sea of other blonde-haired, blue-eyed Alice-hopefuls and their mothers.

Mom and I picked up our form to fill out and turn in for my audition, and then I noticed the awkward dance of the audition—something that never seems to change. Everyone was smiling at each other, somewhat sympathetic that we all knew each other's pain, and somehow trying to size up what was going on behind our strained and nervous acknowledgments.

She's too chubby for Alice...but maybe she's like this unbelievable gymnast or singer or maybe her dad knows the chairman of the board. And that girl...well, she's definitely in the running, but maybe the director is tired of the same old perfect-for-the-part actress. Maybe I should have worn my hair to the left. What if I have a tickle in my throat when I have to read...what are we reading? What if my face does that tic thing it does when I'm scared? Where is the bathroom...and how fast can I make it to the door and out of here altogether?

These thoughts always whirl like a merry-go-round through one's brain at an audition. It's like spinning a roulette wheel and hoping the ball will land on "shaken but confident" by the time you have to go onstage in front of all the other people—people watching who are secretly hoping you'll trip or throw up or do something terribly embarrassing during your chance in front of the director.

Auditions are a nightmare.

But as an 11-year-old novice, I was still too young and clueless to be terrorized by the ordeal, and so when my name was called I got up and did a pretty passable audition. The director, Charles, was a man of amazing patience and gentleness—just the type for directing a young theater company. He asked me about my experience, and like a fool, I gave him an overview of *Lonely Helena* like it was *Macbeth*. But he never laughed or made me feel silly.

And so I made it through the first round all the way to a callback audition where it was down to five of us. We finalists sweated through the same process on another day, then went home to wait for the phone to ring.

A day passed in silence. Never have I wanted so much for a telephone to ring. But it didn't, and I went to bed despondent, sure I had lost the role to someone else, perhaps the 16-year-old who had played Maid Marian in a production of *Robin Hood*.

Mom rushed into my room the next morning, barely able to contain herself. "Bonnie, you have a call," she announced. I ran to the phone. "You have been chosen to be Alice for us!" the theater lady chirped. Inside I skyrocketed. And theater became my dream.

The entire eight weeks of rehearsal and performance was a launching, learning time for me. I was surrounded by kind and giving actors and actresses who had done many productions. I was the only child. The director took me by the hand and taught me stage directions, etiquette, and other theater tricks and allowed me to bring my own skills into the magic that became this play. I have vivid memories of the first day he blocked a scene and wrote in the inside cover of my script where center stage, stage right, stage left, upstage, and downstage were. He taught me the fundamentals and repeatedly told me how important my concentration would be. What I remember most is how much he encouraged me simply by telling me I could do it. If he said it, then I acted on his faith in me.

Of course, there were a couple of hitches. During the first week of production I got a stomach virus, and mom took me to get a shot that would keep "Alice" from hurling all over the little kids in the audience. I was very woozy and weak in the knees, but I got through the performance by using various tricks, like having one of the characters hop onstage with a wet cloth. I worked it into the scene by first trying to take a bite out of it, then finally using it to mop my brow.

All in all, I was completely impassioned by the experience. I loved the smell, taste, feel, and magic of being a character in a play. I'd found my fire in the belly, something I knew I was gifted for, and this fever and fire has never diminished. The first time I went to New York, I was 18, and I saw the closing night of Angela Lansbury in *Gypsy* at the Wintergarten Theater. When I walked into the historic auditorium, I felt like I was 11 years old again. Chills ran over me and tears fell down my face for the entire performance. I was swept into a world where men and women bring stories of human experience to life in a way that will always thrill and fascinate my soul.

For years I believed my destiny would be to move to New York, study acting and musical theater, and enter that world professionally on whatever level I could compete. I did go to New York at age 19 and sang in a Top-Forty show group to earn the money to study. I never studied. I returned home after a year on the road, tired and weary and still full of a dream unrealized.

But God had other plans for me. He allowed me the great experience of acting and singing for many years afterward in local productions of wonderful plays and musicals. And He groomed me, letting me use the same skills required in theater to communicate His truth and faithfulness to His people for His purposes and seasons. I welcomed this unforeseen path with many questions, but I was still grateful to be able to find my way to a stage so I could reach people in the way I'm best equipped to reach them. Only this time I was able to incorporate the writing and sharing of my deepest experiences—maybe not through theater, but in a way that God used far beyond what I might possibly have pursued just for my own ego.

I remember that for years I would lie facedown on the floor at certain times during the week and pray specifically for

God to show me what to do with my passion for the arts. For a while, I did some on-camera commercials. I modeled. I sang in clubs. I did studio work and community theater and wondered where in the "wide world of sports" I would land.

God was faithful to allow me to grow up with Him as I learned the finer points of singing and speaking. It wasn't until I was 24, however, that I discovered Christian music existed. And suddenly there I was, immersed in my lifelong dream of writing, singing, traveling, and expressing this miracle of who Christ is, touring with Amy Grant, Russ Taff, and Sandi Patty. How do you top starting out by watching and learning from artists such as these? Sometimes I have to thank God over and over again for allowing me such rare experiences. I pray none of them have been wasted. And I pray that my own group's legacy will be one of inspiration to younger groups—to groups that love harmony and love to push the envelope a bit by trying some rather different harmonic gymnastics.

A great friend once told me, "God never gifts people to frustrate them. Just wait on His time and will to reveal itself." And so I go to the theater now for pure joy. Occasionally I am lucky enough to be in a production if my schedule allows. And I am writing theatrical pieces for video that I use in my solo concerts and speaking events, which incorporate some of the history and love I have of the craft of "make-believe."

Deep down, I'm breathing in every second of it, thanking God for how He uses each of us wherever we are most useful.

Alice is still in me...that little girl who searched for magic in dreams and colored lights and in the journey of human experience in places new and unfamiliar and exciting. The last line I had in that wonderful first performance came after Alice woke under the tree with her older sister (played by Maid Marian) and realized she'd been asleep. I reached my hand into my pocket, pulled out a glove from the White Rabbit, looked out into the audience, and asked, "Or was it a dream?"

It still is.

The Preacher

~

Our preacher was well-versed in Greek. He could speak Greek and used Greek analogies when preaching to his little southern, white, middle-class auditorium of people who must have felt like he was speaking Greek every Sunday.

I never understood a thing he said. He scared me. Pasty white, never smiling, he looked like he had stepped right out of a wax museum. I thought if anyone ever told him something real they were thinking, he might spontaneously combust right there on the spot.

But everybody kept saying he was worthy because of the Greek. He was smart, so I heard, because he knew Greek. Yippee. I pinched myself silly to stay awake and hear his Greek analogies and Greek interpretations of all kinds of interesting things like why we should or shouldn't go and see the movie *Jesus Christ Superstar*. Or why we should or shouldn't play cards, dance, or have anything to do with Elvis.

The preacher said that by age 12 everyone needed to be baptized. This was because Jesus taught in the temple at age 12, so it followed that one must become able to really sin—sin the sins that count—at age 12. Oh, dear! I knew that somewhere in heaven there was a slate that had my name on it, and when I turned 12, a kind but detail-oriented angel would begin writing down all the bad things I might do, keeping track of exactly where I was to be positioned in hell.

And so in August of 1967 I walked down the aisle of my church and was baptized with my best friend Kathy. Both of us were age 12. Whew! Just in the nick of time. That afternoon,

I remember thinking my slate had been erased. My sweet angel had taken a celestial eraser and had wiped off the horrid things I'd done up to that point. I had a clean slate. For at least that one day in August. The rest of my life seemed up for grabs.

What no one bothered to explain in English—or in Greek— was that God's grace would envelop and love me through the rest of my life. I never heard the message that Jesus died for everyone's desperate state. And that no matter how much we failed ourselves and Him, the miracle of the whole thing was that His love knew no bounds, no constraints.

I lived in constant fear and terror of God's love for many years. It wasn't until I went to college that I had a Bible professor who wisely challenged me to study the life of Job. In this study, the doors of my heart opened and God's Holy Spirit poured in. Jesus' being began to be defined through my haze of fear, and His personhood and godhood became vibrant, vivid, and searing.

Slowly my passion for music and theater and all of the uncharted places that beckoned me to follow the Yellow Brick Road began to take shape in my soul. I had discovered the divinity and humanity of a God whose love I could not fathom.

Today I am grateful to have grown up in a church that loved God in spite of the box in which it placed Him. And I know now that God uses the heart of a child whose disappointment lies in not seeing a magical moment here on earth. He infuses these hearts with the courage, the wisdom, and the love of good things that have been His to give from the beginning. These are the truths I imagine the preacher must have wanted me to know, the truths he was trying to get across before the Greek got in the way. It is these characteristics of God's grace that have seen me through the valleys of despair and into the places of peace I now know.

These are truths in any language.

Fierce Intentions

~

My grandmother left me her name, Bonnie, and the impression that loving God must be a fierce and passionate pursuit. It had to be fierce because God was fierce—and fairly impatient on top of that. Grann's intense faith was genuine, heart and soul. And she felt it was her duty to let me know I needed to please God...or else. A relationship with God and acceptance of Christ as my Savior were a matter of life and death—which is true, of course. However, her version of finding God didn't include knowing His great mercy, His great grace given through the heart—His Son, and then resting in the Holy Spirit—Christ's gift to us for guidance, counseling, and relief.

Grann's idea of pursuing God was to live your life like you were walking a tightrope. If you fell to one side or the other, losing your balance for some reason, it was your fault. God would have no choice but to sadly send you packing. Church attendance was important, like punching a time clock at work. If you were there, then you were in a safety zone. You needed to be in church three times a week or once again God would turn His back. Grann didn't talk of being at church out of love for God or out of need for fellowship; it was more a way to keep from being doomed to perdition. She loved God and Jesus and worked hard at this love, just like she worked hard all her life on the farm she and Papa lived on, lovingly raising their three children. But she had a hard way of loving that never felt comforting to me. For her view of life was sharp, precise, and unforgiving. It threatened me, a skinny girl, all legs with a mess of blonde hair.

Grann was, however, a wonderfully interesting, true-blue character. We loved to laugh at her because her strengths were so out front and in-your-face and she cared not whether you agreed with her opinions on things—she *knew* she was right, so you just needed to get over it! She was practical to a fault. At my first wedding ceremony, she looked at my younger brother, who was in his early twenties at the time, and said matter-of-factly, "That's a pretty bridesmaid you came down the aisle with. Why don't you just turn around, go back down the aisle, and make this a double wedding? We've all had our baths."

One of my favorite memories is Grann at a Christmas gathering, proudly announcing her purchase of a fabulous, brand-new girdle and how much she loved wearing it. When everyone howled, she lifted her dress to show us with a startled "gotcha!" smile on her face, which of course made it worse! But, no question, she was the matriarch of our family and a powerhouse of faith—a sort of rousing, camp-meeting-on-the-grounds, hellfire-and-damnation preacher in an apron (and a great girdle).

Grann would sit me down at an early age and tell me about the Lord. Most of the talk frightened me, as the laws about following God sounded so very much like the Greek-speaking preacher at my home church. God has rules. Be perfect as He is perfect. That's what the Greek preacher said, too. Just do it. *But how?* I had migraine headaches from the time I was six years old until I was in my mid-twenties, and I think some of it came from my trying to figure out this perfection thing. My divorce, depression, and single parenting years clearly taught me that my imperfections were the very reason I needed what Grann was talking about.

As a child, I knew I wasn't perfect, though I tried my best and hardest to please. And I knew Grann knew the Bible better than anyone. She could faultlessly quote long passages of Scripture. Before she died, she even wrote out in her own words the high points of God's Word as she saw them. Each of her children and grandchildren received a copy—her way of making sure that after her death, as in childhood at her knee, we could count on a point being made about God's will and ways, and possibly expect some sort of test to come later.

She and I had our own sort of tests, played out like games (I somehow think she and the Greek-scholar preacher at home in Nashville had planned this whole thing). As soon as I could read, she would sit me down and drill me on how fast I could find the books in the Bible. "Now, Bonnie," she'd say kindly, "when I say so, I want you to open the Bible and as fast as you can find...Malachi...okay...go!"

Pages flying, I'd hunt for this book that sounded like a foreign country. After a while, I got good at it. Within seconds, I could land my hands on any of the Bible's 66 books, including the weirdest-sounding ones—Nahum, Habakkuk, Zephaniah, Haggai. I took pleasure in knowing the proper order of the books, yet no one ever talked about what was in them. In general terms, I was basically told that the Old Testament wasn't too relevant anymore and the New Testament was where the story really started. But being able to quickly find these books earned Grann's approval, and this fit into the teachings I had learned to try to decipher at home, after my baptism and into my teenage years.

I have great memories of staying with Grann for certain weeks in the summer. I would awaken in the farmhouse she shared with my quiet, sweet Papa to the smell of her biscuits, cocoa, butter, and sugar turnovers. Then I'd play with her colorful dishes on the porch. She and Papa called it "the homeplace." Their relationship was simple and solid. One of the greatest things she ever said to me was when she was in her seventies and looked me in the face one day with a smile and said, "Even now, when your Papa touches my hand, I tremble." And so it was to their homeplace, just outside of Gallatin, Tennessee, that the results of those tremblings and their children as well would find their way back on holidays and occasionally throughout the year.

I didn't especially enjoy the preaching Grann doled out, although she did come by it naturally. Her father was a well-known preacher in North Carolina who must have drilled her in the same format she carried on with gusto. I respected her and she always greeted us all with open arms, love, and kisses. But there were just certain things I never brought up around Grann for fear of the hellfire sermon that would inevitably come.

The greatest part about gathering at Grann's was that Grann could cook! She was one of the greatest southern cooks I've ever known. She always had mounds of food prepared and would walk around with a huge spoon while we ate, refilling our plates and insisting we needed just a little bit more. One had to love her readiness to feed thundering hordes of relatives, neighbors, churchgoers, and anyone who had the good fortune to land on her doorstep around dinnertime. It was best to go visit Grann with an empty stomach because you'd have plenty of opportunity to "have just a little more, now—or you'll waste away!"

Maybe this reverence for food came from living through the Great Depression, when she and Papa raised three children on the wages from his job at the railroad station. Or maybe it came from her strict upbringing and, as the oldest of ten children, carrying a heavy load of responsibilities early in life. In any case, Grann learned to always keep her apron handy and to have something fabulous on the stove.

In the later years of her life, our family gatherings took place on Memorial Day weekend at my uncle's home. There would be tables set up with food that everyone knew would please Grann and Papa. Like a queen on her throne, Grann would sit in a large, comfortable chair and observe the legacy she had birthed—all the children, cousins, and grandchildren, swatting mosquitoes together and laughing. At the last gathering where she was present, I was in the middle of a crisis in my marriage and did not tell Grann about it, knowing it would break her heart. It was better for her not to know about my pending divorce...she most assuredly would have gone to heaven uncertain that I'd meet her there.

As I look back now, I see how God honored the fierce intentions of my Grann's heart. I call it "that generational blessing thing." I picture her in heaven, looking down now and saying, "Oh, please forgive me for some of the rigid rules I imposed on you...I was a bit off here and there." And I imagine she is laughing out loud that in God's great irony, He has me singing in all kinds of churches all over the world where loving Christ is the common thread that overrides any differences in approaching Him. I guess too that even some eternal work was done by the efforts of the well-meaning preacher back home. God's words never bounce back empty-handed.

These fierce intentions were seeds planted in me—seeds of desire to discover what lay behind this fierce loyalty and commitment. My heritage from my church and from my family lit a fire in me that continues to burn. Through my personal tests and journey, I now have discovered my own fierce intentions to know God more fully each day and to reflect the grace Christ died for. For that, there is no way to thank enough the ones who came before me and led me here.

Keeping the
Monsters at Bay

~

It's no earth-shattering big deal for a child to be afraid of the dark. It's no novel phenomenon for a child to believe that oogly-ugly monsters wait in her closet at night for the lights to go out so she can be eaten in one mighty gulp. And so, like most every other kid out there, I faced bedtime with uncertainty and anxiety.

Mixed into my overeager imagination and fear of the sun going down was a strongly ingrained combination of fearful theology and a message that I must be a pleaser. My Vacation Bible School lessons at church left no doubt in my mind that if I didn't do things a certain way, God couldn't possibly love me. In fact, I hold no fond memories of VBS. It's just a collage of grape Kool-Aid, hot summer days in the South, and lessons that seemed void of the cool breezes of grace that I longed for. The people must have meant well, but to this day I break out in a sweat at the mention of VBS activities. I threaten my children that I will take them to VBS as punishment if they push me too hard.

What kind of mother am I, anyway?

I guess I'm the kind who looks back at many elements of my wonder years with a healthy respect for the price tag that came with the expectations I placed on myself and that were given to me both consciously and subconsciously by my family and my religious culture.

I've dissected some of the root causes that left me a candidate for depression and despair. This is not to blame my past or to lay the consequences of my own journey at the feet of anyone but myself and my choices. But in stepping back and taking a larger overview of my life, I can put together the pieces of the puzzle and figure out what made me a rabid people-pleaser, someone terrified of failure.

Being left with the impression that God's love was conditional created an imaginary person in my head. As an adult, I've named this person Lois Millblocken. I named her after the Scripture verse about how causing someone to stumble by your example—in my case, divorce, failure, debt, dating badly—would leave you better off having the Mafia roping a millstone around your neck and throwing you into the river than ever facing God with such a history.

Lois grew up inside of me, but she really started in full-steam ahead during my single parenting/divorce recovery period. I don't think she wanted me to recover. The whole healing process deeply offended her, and I'm glad to say that now she's only a faint, irritating, whining little woman who I lock in a special room in my head when she acts up. But when I was a teenager and a young adult, Lois had me convinced that if I behaved well enough, then maybe God just might let me slip into heaven on a wing and a prayer. And this did not sit well with me—body or soul.

My mom was the product of an even more severe church background and even more severe expectations, raised with a "spare the rod and spoil the child" message by her own overbearing mother. Mom was often disciplined for little reason and was tutored from birth that she must do the same if she wanted to be a responsible parent.

Along came me—the first child of my family—and I was given what all first children get from their parents (as my own daughter often reminds me): the expectation of great achievement with minimal resistance. Again, it was a spoken and unspoken eleventh commandment that "one does not question authority." And I was so full of questions! I still am!

My questions did not sit well with my mom—body or soul. She was a woman passionate with her love and passionate with her discipline. I remember being physically disciplined for lots and lots of things without understanding a great deal of the reasons behind the punishment. And I can just hear Lois cheering my mother on as she kept me "in line." I wasn't drinking or smoking or being sexually active or shoplifting or hurting small animals or doing any heinous thing that would be on Lois' list. But I must have been doing something terribly wrong. I wasn't doing enough to please God, my family, or myself. So I kept asking questions. There were too many things that didn't line up. I made A's and B's in school, lived in terror of asking the wrong question or stepping out of line, and yet was continually punished for not submitting to something I couldn't define.

I remember being at the dinner table one evening at Grann's house with my parents and other assorted relatives. I must have been wearing a questioning look, or maybe I said something to set off mom. All of a sudden she glared at me, and without thinking, my younger brother and I both flinched, ready for a "spare the rod, spoil the child" episode. Grann sat there complacently, as if this were the correct reaction for children to have towards their parents (which spoke volumes about how she viewed discipline). But mom's younger sister got on her soapbox about how terrified we were of mom and how we reacted instinctively in fear when we displeased her.

There then ensued a wonderful, alive—yet somewhat disturbing—interchange between my mom and her sister, which ended in mom leaving the table terribly hurt. Our family is dramatic, and there's never been a shortage of feelings to go around like leftovers. But the feelings that stand out for me are the fear of being wrong...and the fear of displeasing...and the fear of asking.

At home, in the dark, I made peace with the monsters in my room—the ones under the bed and in the closet—by entertaining them. I would please them by being clever and sweet. At night, I'd sit up in my purple organza canopied bed and visualize the monsters standing around me. They were sort of my own version of the *Where the Wild Things Are* creatures—kind of cute, but drooling, ready to bite into me if I didn't keep them happy. I would talk and laugh and keep them at bay by tap-dancing my way through a myriad of little jokes and songs and enchanting bits of amusement.

When my parents were not at home during the day, I would play the piano to keep the monsters from having me for an afternoon snack. I convinced myself that if I played the piano, they would love me and not hurt me. I played for hours (time which didn't go to waste) until I got up the courage to run out the back door into the yard until my parents returned. I made peace with the monsters by performing.

So performing...and growing up afraid to ask questions...and because of the messages that came through to me about music and what was expected and not allowed and then occasionally applauded...left me having to release the tension somehow. Journals held a safe, coveted, private haven for me at an early age. When I was punished...or fearful...or ill...or feeling the worst possible feeling—anger...I would go into my room and close the door and tear into my journal. More than once I tore pages apart in a rage I couldn't express anywhere else. I wrote out things I longed to shout or say or ask. These journals were the deepest, most vulnerable expressions of my heart. I also had headaches and threw up a lot.

I believe that each one of us reacts to situations differently, according to how God has wired us emotionally. What caused me physical nausea and pain might easily have rolled off someone else. But I was and am tightly wound, and later on became easily unwound.

Wrestling down the monsters as an adult has been easier for me since I discovered the grace of Christ. He knows I'm tightly wound, and that Lois needs to die a slow, torturous death, and that in the end all the things that make up a person—good, bad, and ugly—are forgiven through His blood. (Oh, how I love to say His name—Jesus—because it's so terribly politically incorrect!) But in Jesus' name I am able to understand how His mercy is the greatest gift I can give to myself and to all the elements of my past that have made me who I am today. It's the life raft I can try to pass on to my children. And with grace, I can see how I have failed those who have been close to me. I can see how two people can fail each other for so long that, short of a miracle, lives are separated, wounds grow gangrenous—and yet the mercy of the cross survives.

The grace of God, like a litany, once again comes to me.

As a parent myself, I have struggled with many things, discipline being one of the weakest areas for me. Afraid of being too strict, I've been much too giving, and subsequently my children and I wade through different challenges of communication than did my mother and I. Mom says I exaggerate. Maybe so. But I know that every path continues to lead me to the door of grace—with me beating and pounding, and pleading with a God who loves me in spite of how I fail and the questions I ask. He meets these failings. His presence silences the pain that I will not understand this side of heaven.

So I will give my children something different to write about when they grow up. At least we can ask together and struggle to work out our salvation with much fear and trembling. And this is the kind of fear that doesn't overwhelm but rather somehow comforts.

My mom and I ask some hard questions now and cry and pray together. I've seen God move and change us both to bring us closer to Him by taking us kicking and screaming to our knees. He's closer in all the uncertainty than I ever imagined. And who knows but our dearest Savior what waits around the next corner.

One
COLORS

Two
RED

Three
ORANGE

Four
YELLOW

Five
GREEN

Six
BLUE

Seven
PURPLE

Eight
RAINBOW

Life breaks us all sometimes in unexpected ways, but some of us grow strong in the broken places.

—Ernest Hemingway

January, 1990

   Had a succession of nightmares last night. The last one was of us all being caught in a rainstorm. My husband left to get our son, Graham. We still had to find our daughter, Courtney, and had many levels of a parking garage to go through—we lost our car—and finally I ran to where Courtney was. She was standing with my grandmother. In the process, my husband showed up pushing a baby carriage—it was black and empty. I asked where Graham was and he said he'd given Graham to a girl who said she would bring him to us. I panicked and ran into the rain to try and find this girl who had my son...woke with my heart pounding...haunted most deeply by the image of the empty baby carriage.

March, 1990

   I couldn't sleep at all last night—preoccupied with this feeling that Daniel has someone else in his heart and life now. It feels crazy to think this, but he's so distant and sad and nothing feels right about where we are. I thought things were getting better but something is terribly, terribly wrong....

April, 1990

   Had a dream—all the electricity went off in our house at night. I asked my husband to please get a flashlight but I ended up doing it alone. Trying to rescue...

April, 1990

   Russ and Tori prayed for my shattered marriage yesterday, Palm Sunday—I'll never forget it. Mom and dad were absolute class. The last thing daddy said was for me to gain some weight and take care of myself and the children—just let go and let God minister to my husband now. I needed to hear that, for to take on the complete responsibility for the betrayal feels like a bottomless pit to me. Yet I do feel like a failure, and I must deal with the part I played in leaving him to feel he needed to move outside the marriage for companionship.

April, 1990

So sad today. Such grief. This marriage is dead. What comes now may be a rebirth—who knows—but this is just death. The death of trust, the death of monogamy, the death of innocence, and just such grief.

April, 1990

I feel so bad, so guilty…wondering what else I have done…if only I had…

May, 1990

Driving to the grocery, crying and praying, pleading with God to help me…As I felt this pain again, it slowly subsided as I had a sense of God impressing on my heart that if I was worth dying for and being reconciled to Him, then I couldn't be all bad! If God feels I have priceless value, then any man's treatment of me should be kept in perspective.

August, 1990

Funny…I always thought of divorce as a chicken-hearted, easy, lazy choice for a weak, pathetic person…and now I'm that person. At church today the sermon was on walking in faith—expanded faith—and believing Jesus will be there as we walk, with His arms outstretched, saying "Come," whether we have failed or not. I must not define my faith by my marital status. I will not leave or be left by God either way…I am not divorcing my faith!

September, 1990

From reading *Inside Out* by Larry Crabb: "God has not kept His distance. He deals with life as it is, not as we wish it was. If we desire to meet Him and to taste His loving presence we must open our eyes to whatever is true, however unsettling it may be."

October, 1990

I cannot believe I live day after day moving toward divorce. I am so very lonely, so desperately sad at watching my marriage close. Final chapter...I am painfully aware of my humanity. Jesus, help me.

November, 1990

How in the world did I end up here? In Manila, the Philippines, after a 16-hour flight and after signing the final divorce papers the night before we left? I miss my babies so much...and my Grann is dying...I've never felt as low, tired, empty, and afraid all at the same time...yet I can't turn back. I have to believe God has not let go of me.

November, 1990

Eleven years ago I woke up, dressed, ate, and went to a lovely church on a cold, clear day and got married. Today, 11 years later, I woke up in Singapore—alone, afraid, very sad—and somehow going on with my life. I thank God for my children—they are the sweet joy of my life and my reason to stay strong.

November, 1990

Arrived home after this exhausting trip. I miss the good part of what my husband and I "could have" had. I experienced all over again the loss of our broken dreams and realized with intense pain that I can never trust him again. At the airport we cried—all of us, our fractured family. The children were rich medicine for my grief—precious, sweet, unadulterated love. I saw them coming and ran down the jetway and we fell on each other. My husband and I hugged politely and sadly cried. I was so dizzy and faint and tired, no anger anymore, just numb.

TWO

January, 1991

I am beginning to taste a new discovery—forgiveness. As I read in Carolyn Streeter's book, "One reason forgiveness is so essential for you is that you have a future. You will not be able to walk into the kind of future God has in mind for you if you do not first experience this sense of wrongs made right, of burdens lifted, of dirty places cleansed, of unacceptable made acceptable." I have spent so much time with self-discovery that I've missed the whole point of my faith—forgiveness! Self-discovery is fine—but far better yet is daily absolution!

April, 1991

Had a pivotal conversation today where I found out there is definite talk of marriage happening for my soon-to-be ex-husband. He is continuing the relationship with her on serious terms and in front of people that he respects and works with, which is a serious public statement of his future intentions. I suppose there should be some relief in knowing I haven't imagined the torn place he's in. It hurts. So many of our friends are grieving this too, which is a whole separate pain to deal with. My sweet Courtney knows. With her "wise eyes," she keeps watching us and crying, and I know this will be so very hard for her. As the afternoon wears on, it all continues to sink in. My children with a stepmother...my place in this marriage forever gone...acceptance comes slowly.

May, 1991

Somehow my faith in God has remained through this fire. I do not fear a loss of faith but a loss of myself.

September, 1991

God can teach me in the pain, can reach me, can touch me in this pit. His presence is not often palpable or even soothing. I can look back and see how I have had the strength to survive not on my own but in Him. Right now, it feels like it's just a decision to believe, a willingness of my heart to trust that God holds me, that even now He loves me. So often I don't know whether I really believe anything anymore. I feel somewhat left to the winds of chance. I hate the doubt, and wonder whether I so offended God's Holy Spirit that I am living outside of His care. Yet I see mercy in my life—in my children's lives—although I am afraid of being punished for this divorce. Help me, God, please, to hear Your voice in this most horrible of times.

October, 1991

Signed the final divorce papers today. I don't believe it. What a strange, deathly quiet in my heart. It was a rainy, foggy, dark day, totally the opposite of the sunny, crispy cold day in November when I gave my vows to my husband twelve years ago. What a horrible, unnatural process—this ripping apart. The two of us did become one and this is a tearing down of what God put together. Yet how to stay in this marriage now? God, please forgive me for the qualities in me that made it seem impossible for him to stay. I prayed before I left the lawyer's office for one more sign to stop this process...and for forgiveness and strength and healing for us all.

October, 1991

The divorce was final on Friday. I half expected my husband to come into the courtroom and stop it all. There were twinges of sadness for our lost dreams and a stillness all day. As I went to bed, sad, tired, and afraid, I also felt a strong and real presence of Jesus' arms around me—and a deep sense of being comforted.

Healing flows like a river
It was scarlet love that He bled
And the world was changed like black to white
With every drop of red

—Bonnie Keen and Lowell Alexander, from "Drop of Red"

"Broken Places"

Lay down your weary head when the troubled waters flow
Life breaks us all sometimes where we need to grow
Innocence is not a crime, in time we understand
And find the grace of mercy slipping through
the fingers of God's hand

I know the broken places, I can name them one by one
Sown in the spaces, the seed of work left to be done
Each wound the heart embraces becomes
a cry that God has won
And He knows the broken places

He treasures every tear
In a jar of alabaster
He'll use to wash away the years

The years of broken places
And with His love He traces
Each wound the heart embraces
becomes a witness to someone.

—Bonnie Keen, Darrell Brown, and Tori Taff, from "Broken Places"

Numb

~

Holy Father God, hear the prayer of your divorced children,
to create in us a clean heart. Renew a right
spirit in us. Cast us not away from Your presence at this time of
failing and defeat. Rather let our broken bones learn to sing of
Your grace, and grant unto us Your everlasting mercy. Heal the
many broken places in our hearts and lives,
to Your glory and in the name of our only Savior, Jesus, amen.

—BASED ON PSALM 51

I felt twinges of nausea in the pit of my stomach as I sat in the waiting room of our marriage counselor's office. Not once in all the many sessions Daniel and I went through—sometimes we went to three sessions a week—did I not have a feeling of helpless weakness as we waited. The hanging plants and wicker furniture looked so strangely cheerful. Everyone in the waiting room sat in silence, as if waiting to have our teeth drilled without novocaine. Pieces of paper advertising divorce recovery groups and the like were tacked up to a bulletin board. I tried to ignore them. Stacks of news magazines sat on a table. I was afraid to touch them for fear I would lose my concentration for the session ahead.

Every time I went to the counselor's office, I would pray, asking God to speak through the time we had, asking Him to give me the courage to be honest and to hear Daniel's heart. Knees shaking, my heart would lurch right on cue as the counselor walked down the creaky stairs and into the waiting room to greet us.

We'd been seeing our marriage counselor for eight months when I learned that I needed immediate surgery to remove a precancerous area of my body. After finding out this news, we talked with our counselor about the situation, discussing Daniel's role in taking care of Courtney and Graham while I was in the hospital.

In this particular session, our counselor seemed pleased. He smiled at us and said he thought we were over the hump with the work we had done. He told us that each couple he sees has a body of work to do, and when it is accomplished it's time for them to move on. I too felt that the time of waiting was over—that Daniel and I had been through torturous conversations and confessions and had come to a new place in our marriage. These were the first feelings of optimism I'd experienced in a long time, and I hoped we would be able to move on to the marriage God had intended us to have all along.

I was wrong.

The day of my surgery, my best friend, Tori Taff, took me to the hospital. In spite of my fears and the atmosphere of this cold green-and-white room, Tori's loving wit kept me laughing. The nurse came in and gave me a "horse shot" to calm me down for the trip to the operating room. Tori's husband Russell came in to encourage me, joining Tori in keeping things light and optimistic. Finally Daniel arrived. He alone walked with me as they rolled my bed to the elevator that would take me to the operating room, and his face looked strangely grieved.

Several days later, sleeping in a downstairs room while I recovered at home from the operation, I woke up and said out loud, "Daniel is in love with someone else."

There was no preparation for this. I believe the Holy Spirit was gently readying me for a hard truth. I talked to my husband and discovered he did have strong feelings for someone else—believed he was truly in love with her, in fact.

The pieces of many unexplainable circumstances came together. Everything in our world fell apart.

Early in the morning, we talked about the separation, the moving out, the failure of our marriage. We quietly talked, cried, and negotiated in a room where I had been staying while we were apart in the house—a room we had added on while I was pregnant, a room where he had arranged a surprise birthday party for me, a room where I had realized my husband and I were no longer one.

We sat in the dawn of a spring morning in front of the windows that looked out over our backyard, a place where all the neighborhood kids would gather to play, and wondered where Daniel would go. I felt suddenly, strangely numb, as if I were watching myself from somewhere far away. Then we walked into the kitchen, where I packed my husband a "going away" lunch in a brown paper bag, like he was one of the children. I did this despite my vow to break one of the bad habits I had brought into our marriage—the habit of taking care of a grown man who needed to take care of himself.

He left.

One night Daniel came by to see the children. Courtney was playing the piano while Graham danced, running around in circles until the music stopped. It was surreal and empty and scary that our children did not realize their father wouldn't be around to see everyday moments like these anymore. As we watched our children play, we tried to play out the song of acceptance for our own situation.

The first time Daniel came to take the kids to his apartment, he had to perform the strange act of ringing the doorbell to a house he used to enter freely. And while all of us tried to pretend this was doable, the air around us screamed otherwise. Two-year-old Graham, dimpled hands around his father's neck, was blissfully unaware he wouldn't see me for two days. But six-year-old Courtney's wise eyes were full of tears. She tried to be brave, but she made it halfway down the sidewalk and then ran back into my arms, crying.

I watched his car drive away with the three of them, and I bravely waved at the window until they were out of sight.

And, placing my broken heart at the feet of Christ, I waited for them to return.

Broken Places

≈

I am a five-foot-eleven blonde who can have the semblance of looking fairly together, as those outward kinds of things go. I've spent the majority of my professional life onstage, communicating through theater and music about my faith with a God-given confidence. Most of the time I'm grateful for these gifts. But sometimes I worry that people will look at me and say to themselves, "Hey, this divorce thing seems to have worked out pretty well for her. She looks just fine. Maybe divorce isn't such a bad option after all."

Hold the phone! Let me be completely clear on this one thing: No one but the Lord can know about the many ugly nights I spent on the floor, crying out to Him, praying for any morsel of hope I could hold on to that would keep me from wanting to die...or from giving up on my faith...or from letting the intense fear of single parenting overwhelm me.

I most certainly do believe that divorce is a tragedy. And it is not the will of our Father God for us. But in this world of free will, with spouses free to choose directions to move into or out of and all sorts of private, painful situations that abound behind closed doors, I believe that divorce is sometimes the least destructive and unfortunately—for some of us—necessary choice between bad and worse.

When I looked at the paper that pitted my husband and me against each other—Keen vs. Keen, it read—I shook. How in the world did I end up here? How could God ever reach me in this broken place? How could I possibly minister to others when my life was in such shambles?

I'd always been a person who thought she could make things work. If there was only enough sacrifice, if only I could jump through just the right hoops, if only I could die to myself in Christ, the right thing would happen. Yet here I was at age 36—a failure at the most basic relationship of my life. Nothing in my legalistic, perfectionist background had prepared me for such a mess.

Interestingly enough, my children were the determining factor in my final decision: that only through a divorce could I live out an honest, God-fearing life before them. That may sound crazy, but as I watched my body and soul fading away in an effort to stay in my marriage, I knew what my decision needed to be. The quest for personal happiness should not be the reason for a divorce. But in some circumstances, children are better served not by a happy parent but by a whole parent. That said, I will also say that children are the best reason to stay and work hard to keep a marriage together, to fight against reaching the point of no return.

A friend of mine who also went through divorce once told me she felt like the church was so preoccupied with keeping families intact that it sometimes lost sight of the fact that, in some situations, restoring the person to the Lord may take precedence over restoring the family. Some marriages may never be healed this side of heaven. But through love and prayer, the fractured people who walk through these broken places can eventually find restoration and healing in the Lord for whatever wounds they carry.

I do know this: God's grace abounds. It is not meant to be taken advantage of, to be used as an excuse for divorce or anything else. But in the end, grace does abound.

If you happen to be contemplating divorce—and if circumstances aren't complicated by a third party's involvement or you or your children aren't being beaten emotionally or physically—and if there's any common ground left to rebuild and work on, I highly urge you to seek wise counsel and hang on.

Let me give you a brief snapshot of what divorce looks like, especially for a single parent.

Dusk is falling, your children are happily playing, and then you realize it's Friday night, which means that your ex will be coming to take them away for the weekend. You pack their clothes, a few toys, their blankets. The children don't understand why they are leaving mom to go with dad, or dad to go with mom. They stand at the door when the doorbell rings and watch you go through the stiff, uncomfortable ritual of handing them over to the other parent and saying, "'Bye—see you in a few days!" You try to smile into their eyes, which are filled with longing or anger or resentment. You go to the window and try not to notice the tears in the eyes of your oldest child in particular, because the oldest always hurts the worst in the beginning. She remembers her parents together, and she knows her world has come apart.

Smiling and waving and choking back a lump in your throat, you watch your fractured family pull out of the driveway. It feels like a knife has pierced your heart. When everyone is out of sight, you fall to the floor and weep until you make those moaning sounds of pain, sounds like you might hear at a funeral. Your life feels like an ongoing funeral where the casket never closes. There is a death, yet never a burial.

Over time, taking your children and leaving them with your ex-spouse and, possibly, his significant other is bearable. At first it's a sheer act of will to walk them to the door of this new house they sometimes stay at. You try to smile, then notice the pictures on the wall—pictures of your children integrated into a new family. A new face looks out at you from the space you used to occupy, and you pray that this person will be kind to and accepting of your children. And then you drive away with no one to drive home to. It takes many years of hurting and asking over and over for grace to find healing and peace.

It has been ten years since my divorce. I am now remarried to a man I adore. And every time my children leave for their father's house, I still cry. God did not intend for families to live this way, although America has made the choice of this path tremendously accessible.

Divorce is serious business, people. And it happens. Sometimes it saves a life—or lives—and sometimes it simply rips things apart and sometimes it's just what comes out in the wash. But oh, the tears and suffering that accompany divorce.

God uses the tears and saves them in that alabaster jar mentioned in the Psalms. The tears are not useless; they mix with Christ's own tears and teach us. But this is still no justification for divorce. So please try hard to make it work. It takes two to try, but it's amazing what pliable, willing hearts can accomplish when they decide there's something still worth fighting for. And even in the ugliest process of anger and rebuilding and cleaning up and starting over, God's grace will unrelentingly abound.

Bridges

~

Anyone who has gone through a separation or divorce knows there are moments when nothing you can do will keep your pain from view. These moments make those around you uncomfortable. Some folks squirm when you bare your emotions, not wanting you to wear too much of your heart on your sleeve, like it is a bad thing for people to know your true feelings. Others might say nothing, but they too don't know how to respond to your hurt, which is strange because pain, like love, is an emotion intense and raw, primal and common. It can make you itch. You don't mind the love so much, but sadness is the rash everyone wants to scratch out—or at least cover up—because it is ugly and confusing. The hows and whys of suffering have never made sense.

When I was going through the separation and then the divorce, there were days, weeks, even years when my emotions lived on the surface, mostly on the faces of my children.

Even now I watch Courtney and Graham as if they are pieces of my heart walking around outside my body. "There's my 16-year-old heart," I tell myself when Courtney wants me to check out her newest outfit (usually a combination of her clothes and mine that end up in the black hole I call her room). When Graham sings at the top of his lungs and sneaks candy from the pantry, I think, "That's my 12-year-old heart racing around outside me." The love I feel for them summons all my instincts to protect them and make them happy, to nurture them and watch them play and rest and relish the everyday things of life, free from worry or fear.

So the complete trust they showed, wide-eyed on Courtney's 11-year-old face and sparkling on seven-year-old Graham's, slammed into me after my marriage unraveled. I recognized their trust but couldn't reflect it, with the betrayals I felt left to wrestle with inside. How could I possibly explain to them how things would go? Feeling confused and beaten by what had transpired, I wasn't sure myself.

"Can this marriage still work?" I had asked myself for years. Finally after a year of counseling and many false starts and stops before that, came the deathly quiet answer in my heart. *No.*

I began to dream ugly scenes—one night a whole succession of nightmares. The nightmares told me something I was beginning to admit: Single mothering was terrifying. It makes you feel like you are losing everything, or like you have become a baby yourself and must grow up all over again with your children, or like you are fumbling about in the dark. In my nightmares, I fumbled alone, trying to rescue the remnants of my family.

One of my greatest fears was that my children might somehow try to shoulder some responsibility for what was happening. "How can I keep them from feeling caught in the middle," I asked my counselor, "or from having to make choices of loyalty toward me or my husband that have nothing to do with the divorce?"

"You're not alone," my counselor reminded me. "You have God and each other, and you are still a family."

Are we? I wondered. The children were so young and ill-equipped to carry this heavy burden of their parents' decisions on their small shoulders. I looked into their innocent faces and began to see shadows of the fears I felt. Most of these glimmers surfaced out of the darkness and safety of their rooms at bedtime. Just before I would call "lights out," their hearts would open with precious vulnerability.

One night, Courtney especially seemed to be having a hard time. On the cusp of that little-girl-to-woman place where you simply can't figure out the whys and hows of your emotions, she had come into my room at bedtime, her ever-aging precious "bankie" in hand, announcing, "Mother, I don't know where to sleep."

I could see on her face the faint flickering of those impending hormones. "You can always sleep with me, baby," I said and stroked her wild hair.

"No! I don't want to sleep in your room!" she stormed, pulling away.

"Are you sure?" I wanted to pull her back close, so that in a time when everything seemed disjointed and out of place, we could lie quietly together and I could stroke her forehead like I did when she was a colicky baby.

"No, Mother!" Her hormones were raging now. "You don't understand!"

"Tell me," I ventured, "why you can't sleep in your own room."

Another hormonal look. "No!"

"Honey..." I started.

But she was flying out of the room, indignant. "I don't know," she said without turning back. "You don't understand."

Then Graham called out from his bedroom. I went in and saw him, so sweet with those blue, blue eyes, and that blonde hair on his pillow. He looked up at me, his beloved "bankie" at his side. "Mommy, I have to ask you something," he said in his most serious voice. "And you have to tell me exactly the truth!"

I looked at him quizzically. "What is it, sweetie?"

"Kathryn told me today there's no tooth fairy. Is that true? Isn't there a tooth fairy in a long pink gown, who lives in a black and purple castle made of painted teeth and comes to our house when I lose a tooth to leave me treats?"

I smoothed his hair, thinking "Kathryn who?" and wondering what to say and who would back me up. "If you believe in a tooth fairy, she can be alive in your heart," I said finally, hoping I'd pulled myself out of a no-win situation.

Faces, like hearts on sleeves, don't lie, and Graham's brows rose in a childish sorrow. "Oh, no!" he wailed. "She's right. There's no tooth fairy!"

Just like a bit of his imagination and innocent dreams, I withered inside as Courtney called from the hall, "Mom! I'm going to bed."

I stroked Graham's cheek. "Give me a minute, honey," I whispered, turning to tuck in Courtney. She had dragged all of the covers and pillows from my bed into the hall and now looked at me, green eyes cloudy and irritable, expecting a reprimand.

"Sweetheart," I said, exhausted and unwilling to battle her on this, "what are you doing?"

"I don't know," she muttered. "You don't understand."

But before I could soothe her fears, before I could tell her that this place of no understanding is one we all seemed to be crossing, Graham called from his room.

"If there's no tooth fairy, then what about the Easter bunny?" he shouted.

I could see where this was headed and wished for reinforcement. There was none.

"It's sort of like the tooth fairy," I braved, "a lovely game we can play."

This time he broke into tears, pools of tears spilling from those blue, blue eyes. "Kathryn said that parents are the Easter bunny and the tooth fairy and it's true! There's no bunny that lives in the bunny kingdom with a big yellow coat and comes and leaves candy baskets for us on the hearth? How could you do this to me?"

Guilt in massive doses rushed through my veins. How could I do this? I couldn't be Supermom. I couldn't even come close. How was I supposed to be both mommy and daddy on nights like this? I suddenly felt very small, alone and afraid of the dark. Courtney wailed again, but not from the hall. I was sinking between my two children, who were crying for me from different shores. Drowning in fear and loneliness, I felt helpless to bring them with me into some boat that would sail into a happier place, a more perfect life where any good thing could happen. Gentle bunnies could rule cheerfully in civilized yellow jackets, and tooth fairies could build something new and shining with all the lost pieces of our lives.

Graham was still crying. I kissed his forehead and turned to tuck Courtney into her makeshift bed in the hallway. I didn't have the strength to force her into her little-girl bed. She could sleep on her pallet and somehow we'd get through the night.

But I found her back in her room, on the floor in the dark, my bedding piled around her like a nest. My little girl—and yet not—almost a young woman now. Unable to find a place to sleep that was comfortable, she lay down between it all: not alone on her little-girl bed or with me in my adult one, but somewhere in between. All the fear for what was coming and all the sorrow for what had passed swirled inside me. I leaned down to kiss her and found under my comforter her faded old blanket, of which she had observed years ago, "I've loved the yellow out of it."

I wanted to linger there, to assure her that love doesn't fade even in the in-between times, but Graham was crying again from his own unsettled place. Here came the big-money question I had been dreading.

"What about Santa Claus?" he wailed.

As I retraced my steps back to his bedside, I imagined finding dear little Kathryn, whoever and wherever she was, and slapping her around in Christian love. While the fleeting idea comforted me, I needed something more lasting for Graham.

"There was once a man in Germany named St. Nicholas," I began, falling into the familiar cadence of a bedtime story, "who left candy for all the children in his village on Christmas Eve. He asked the parents to help him when it became too complicated..."

Graham's eyes pooled again, tears spilling, unstoppable now. "It's true! There's no Santa Claus! All my dreams just hopped out of my heart!"

I wanted to crawl into bed and cry with him, but instead I imagined stepping on little Kathryn—and called for Courtney. She came in and we sat on Graham's bed, together wiping his tears because, I suppose, it was easier than trying to wipe our own.

Exhausted, Graham finally settled under the covers and Courtney went back to her pallet on the floor in her room. I kissed her brave forehead, then sat a while longer with Graham until, drifting off to sleep, he told me, "Mommy, I prayed to Jesus and He told me everything was all right, so all of my dreams hopped back in my heart."

I dragged myself back to my room, marveling at his faith and wondering what was left of mine. I cried for all my lost dreams and all the fallout that threatened to rob my children of theirs. I wanted to yell: "What is happening? My children are crossing these bridges, and I'm scared to death of what to say or do."

I was angry. "God, You didn't create me to raise these children alone, but through the mess and muck of my life, here I am," I prayed. "Where are You in this?" Everything I felt this night was in plain view. I knew it and I knew God could see it, under covers or not. It was daunting enough for two parents, let alone one, to shape the hearts of two small children.

I reached across the bed for someone—Jesus, maybe. I called my mom and my best friend and told them what had happened. Jesus met me in those conversations by offering listening, compassionate ears who'd take such a call late at night. Like Graham, I started to cry myself to sleep, praying not to be left sinking between the dream of what my family was and what I feared it could never be. Somewhere in the crying, between sorrow and frustrated anger, I waited for a reprimand from heaven for all my mistakes in life. For not finding some way to keep my marriage together. For not giving my children more than myself, but a father too. For not being enough to fill all their needs.

Exhausted, I began to drift into sleep. I itched to get beyond this pool of pain, but I was spent of all my tears and hope of answers. That's when I sensed Jesus' whisper: "You're right. You are all crossing bridges, and you can't do this on your own. There will never be enough of you to make it alone, but you're not in this by yourself."

And that's when I began to see that His love would be my way to cross the water.

Drop of Red

~

Where was God when my spouse left me for another woman? Or man? Or job? Or all of the above? Why wasn't God doing something to work some good out of the rebellion in my own heart? If I loved Him, how did this happen? Where has He been, and how can I possibly place my broken, mucked-up life in His hands? How can He be trusted if He has allowed these things to happen? More importantly, where have I been all this time?

If you are like me, you have quite possibly worn out your own ears and those of your best friends or pastor with these demanding questions. These kinds of questions woke me up in the night and tormented me to the point of distraction. Just angry enough to open a can of spiritual worms, I decided to dive into the deepest waters of doubt in an effort to reconcile the inequities of life with the staggering love of God.

Interesting waters—these deep waters of doubt.

Interesting company—these people I found there.

Job. Esther. Mary. Moses. Jonah. David. Countless other men and women of the Bible. As well as many other writers and seekers of these answers. The writings of C.S. Lewis and Frederick Buechner and Martin Luther King, Jr. and Billy Graham articulated so eloquently the issues my heart longed to hear addressed.

Along with awakening to these sources and to the real stories of struggle and despair that God could have omitted from the Bible but did not, I began to listen with different ears to the stories of the men and women God has allowed me to meet over the years. On the road, I met a man who began a prison ministry and brought new purpose to his pain after his son was locked away for armed robbery. I met parents whose children had been stillborn or were challenged with physical or mental conditions. I met parents whose child died at the age of five in a drunk-driving accident. And I listened to the voices of many other single moms who have become bedrocks of encouragement and hope in the midst of unthinkable pain.

Interestingly enough, after awhile spent sitting in the midst of this company, there grew a simple quieting. In the worst of days I began to sense the Lord's active presence—as if He too were crying, walking the floors with us—remaining ever patient as the questions rose and fell from our human hearts. Simple yet unspeakable is the infinite, unmovable love that answers each question.

Over and over again, each question has led me down a path of study and prayer and—sometimes—anger and despair. Yet each path has pointed to the same hill where on a day over two thousand years ago God in the body of Jesus willingly suffered for these very questions. His pain absorbs the doubts. His tears and blood and anger and humanity absorb the tragedy and somehow redeem the loss. His love answers my questions.

Nothing else, no one else—no other book, process, program, or solution—holds up to the cross. Believe me, I have tried many other routes. Each one has had its benefits, and each has contained pieces of the truth. But none could heal the gaping hole left by my divorce. None could touch with a lasting presence the pain, fear of the future, or deep sense of hopelessness. I recall the words of Jesus that took me so long to hear: "I am the way, I am the truth and the life. No man comes to the Father but through me."

Broken Bones

~

I had been divorced for about a year when I found a note in seven-year-old Courtney's room. The quiet, innocent finality in this summation of her young life left me in tears:

My Life
by Courtney Keen

Hi—my name is Courtney Keen. I am seven. And this is my life. On October 11, 1983, the life of Courtney Keen appeared. The doctor that pulled me out pulled too hard and broke my collarbone. Nobody knew it had to grow back together by itself. But I am OK now. From 0 months to 2 years I lived in one place. But the man next door had a motorcycle and rode up and down the street. It bothered me when I was sleeping so we moved to Rolling River and I still live there now. *And my mommy and daddy are parted.*

One of my greatest fears was that Courtney or Graham might somehow try to shoulder responsibility for their parents' parting. Certain as I was that I had to keep my chin up and walk bravely through each day, my faith, self-esteem, and entire outlook on life took a blistering beating. Peace became my heart's greatest desire—peace and a grasping for some assurance that the Lord would not hold this situation against my children.

Singing and ministering in concert was a strange thing for me during this time. I felt guilty and shamed and afraid to speak of my pain—and even more afraid someone would hold the divorce against me and my ministry. Many people who weren't even sure of the circumstances I faced wrote me well-meaning but hurtful letters to confirm my suspicions. In this most desperate time of my life, I felt that God would never call me "daughter" again.

I am not one of those people who hears the Lord speak to me audibly. But I do have impressions from time to time that I believe are the movings of the Holy Spirit—direct leading from God—coming to me through seemingly random conversations, experiences, or readings. And I have taken Scriptures—particularly the Psalms—as my own personal promises from God that He will care for my children.

Many times I've told my kids that I want them to learn from my mistakes, so that when they grow up they can make their own new mistakes. I hope they will see what I have learned the hard way and let it keep them from the same pitfalls. More than anything, I hope they have seen where I have taken my heart when it is broken. As much as I love my children, I know that I cannot prevent the inevitable disappointments that will be a part of their lives. My prayer is that they will know where to take this shade of brokenness that seems to have no answer.

I know that the Lord is clear about His disdain for and hatred of the act of divorce. As much as it hurts to have a failed marriage—or any failure, for that matter—it is also important to read over and over these merciful words from Romans 8: "For I am persuaded beyond doubt...that neither death nor life, nor angels nor principalities, nor things impending and threatening nor things to come, nor powers, nor height nor depth, nor anything else in all creation will be able to separate us from the love of God which is in Christ Jesus our Lord." I would add that neither divorce, betrayal, loss of job, moments of doubt, stupid choices, despair, or depression can keep us from His reach.

The crushing of my bones ushered in the process of dating again, the stress of balancing work and finances and my children's schedules. I had to learn to relate to couple friends as a single person. And I had to deal with physical and emotional weariness and loneliness—new broken places in my soul.

But broken bones do something. They keep you from going anywhere too fast. They force you to lie down, to be still, to listen to God. They give you no other choice.

And I've found there is no better place to be broken than before the Lord. He is tender when you are destroyed. Vulnerability gives God the chance to really love you. How quickly we move through life most of the time, missing so many moments when our Father just wants to hold us. Being broken is a chance to be healed. For me it was a chance to finally lean into those everlasting arms I'd sung about all my life.

Broken bones take time to heal. We want to grow them back together immediately so we can start moving again. But sometimes we need to stay where we are and give them time to grow back together.

One
COLORS

Two
RED

Three
ORANGE

Four
YELLOW

Five
GREEN

Six
BLUE

Seven
PURPLE

Eight
RAINBOW

We're not naturally inclined to love God and seek His kingdom. Trouble may help to incline us—that is, it may tip us over, put some pressure on us, lean us in the right direction.

—Elisabeth Elliot

January, 1994

I feel willing to do whatever God would inspire First Call to do. But where are our hearts? I sense a veil lifting, as our conversations are shifting from being centered on the Lord more onto topics of personal gain…on things that did not initially bring us together. There's nothing wrong with group diversification, yet the spirit now feels like we've come to use each other as a way to further our own personal agendas. God seems strangely in the background…almost incidental.…to have this heaviness when so much healing is coming alive in my heart, especially since the divorce, makes me uneasy. I must seek God's Word and truth to light my path—not walk by the light of my own fires.

January, 1994

Sometimes I feel like First Call is like Moses—we made it through the wilderness but most likely won't walk into the promised land.

January, 1994

Reality is, we don't seem to have a collective heart. Here I am about to leave my children for five weeks to go on a tour where there is potential for an emotional and even physical affair with two people who seem very fragile right now. I know we're all human, but this feels like a bizarre version of Russian roulette.

In contrast to all of this upheaval I feel, God is somehow moving powerfully in my heart right now. I don't think I've ever experienced quite this strong a sense of revelation—revealing. He is revealing Himself, His faithfulness, His will for me, His call for me to trust and to leave Egypt—to walk by faith against the logic of man. Interestingly, Roberta Croteau (editor of *Release* magazine) asked me to write a piece for their next issue. I've been writing on trust—on leaving our own private Egypts of familiar pain and moving in faith to the next place, whatever it might hold. Working on this article has been good therapy for me on this tour.

March, 1994

I feel like I'm watching a collision in slow motion—a collision of lives.

March, 1994

I feel that this group is over for me…like God is calling me to walk on out into the desert. It's like when I was divorced with no man waiting in the wings—there is no career waiting—just God. Only God. I wish I could say I feel filled with a stoic faith, but again I'm scared. The focus in First Call seems torn. The unity is gone. The irony of "Undivided," our first single, is not lost.

April, 1994

I have decided to leave First Call. This weekend I will tell the group and management. I dread hearing "You can't do this now!" but I am resolved to move on.

April, 1994

At the time of this writing, I am sitting backstage after a sound check in Eureka, Missouri. We had a small break and are back together for the first time in a few days. I'll miss so much of this. But…it would feel like death to stay as things are. It strikes me that since my divorce, I've found myself forced to put my entire life piece by piece into the hands of God. First, as a single mother I laid down my womanhood and motherhood, and now it's time to lay down my career.

Easter Sunday, 1994

Agonizing over when to tell Marty of my decision to leave. Today was the perfect day. We flew home together from a concert, just the two of us. I told him the situation was too tense for me to stay. Marty was precious and sad and reflected on his hopes that this situation would right itself before it got worse. I love him like a brother and we both cried a little and spoke of how close we were and how I love Vickie and his boys. Later at home…I told my children. Courtney cried her eyes out about me leaving the group, which set off Graham's tears. I know they don't understand.

April, 1994

"Commit your work to the Lord, then it will succeed."

We did a concert last night, staying at a hotel that's right on the beach of a beautiful inlet. This morning, before we left the hotel, I wanted to see the ocean. I walked out on a boarded pier to the beach and began praising God for the beauty of nature, for the path was surrounded by foliage and lush greenery. I prayed for vision—and thanked Him for His faithfulness. After a while I found myself just talking to Him like I was talking to my best friend, and I was filled with a sense of walking side by side with God, like in Eden—like we were companions, Creator and created. I had a strong sense of His presence and comfort, and then these two sentences passed through me as clear as a voice in my ear: "I am with you. Do not fear." Do not fear what? Fear all that is presently happening, or coming or changing? I have never before felt God speak so clearly to my heart.

April, 1994

What strikes me in the gut tonight is that what's really impor- tant, in the final analysis, is who I am by the end of this life. What will I have done for the cause of right? If First Call's music speaks some sort of hope to people, then should I stay in this, in spite of the cost? Does it mean that I hold my tongue and watch as lives teeter in the balance for the sake of "careers," if it serves a higher purpose? Is my reaction just leftover hurt from my divorce? I called Marabeth's room tonight and left her a message telling her that although we are estranged, I love her and pray for her. We used to be so close, and I feel like I've failed her....

May, 1994 (after the Dove Awards)

Absolute upheaval. God's hand lifted. Mercy, the covering removed. The sin exposed. All hearts break. This is unspeakable.

I keep remembering how some of us were silently weeping and confused during the last week of the tour. Now the wondering is over. All of my agonizing over their behavior seems to have been founded on truth. The last two weeks have been hell—no sleep, media craziness. Marty and I have been like two people planning a funeral, overseeing the estate and trying to deal with our own grief. First Call is devastated, broken, laid bare at the heart and core. We have no record deal. When the news hit, the record company received calls about us and denied having anything to do with us. Booking agency hasn't called. Management is unreachable for the moment. God is laying bare the motive of our hearts. I keep wondering if the real reason this was allowed to play out was that there was much potential for money to be made from certain people's talent—even at the expense of their personal lives. We are all to blame.

May, 1994

It's as if the sky is falling in, down—all is loss and turmoil and grief. *Newsweek* has a picture of Michael and Marabeth— there she is, our beautiful Marabeth. Her beauty seems so violated. I feel such anger at her and anger at myself for not being able to stop her before it got to this.

May, 1994

There's a preacher named E.V. Hill, who summed up where we are now better than I can: "The body of Christ is not made up of clean people, but of dirty people being washed clean by the blood of Jesus. It's not made up of well people, but of sick people, and some of us are getting better one day at a time. It's not made up of straight people, but of crooked people who are being straightened out by the Word of God." That's all of us. That's it. We're all dirty and sick and crooked and by the mercy of Jesus, one day at a time, we're all trying to get better.

The Fine Art
of Fighting

~

I remember one particular spring day in my very white, very
middle-class Nashville neighborhood when I was playing
by myself, making little roads and streets for a phantom city
in the gravel at the end of my very white, very middle-class
driveway. At this particular time in my life, I wasn't aware
that the couple across the street put beer into their baby's
bottle to calm her when her crying got on their nerves. And
it wasn't until years later that my parents explained to me
how they shielded me from the couple next door who occasionally went after each other with knives at night in the heat
of a summer argument. All I knew was that my dad had built
a beautiful fence around our backyard and that my yard
seemed like a haven—safe and green and full of places to
explore. I loved to play in the driveway, creating make-
believe cities with little cars that were parked in make-believe
neighborhoods full of what I suppose were make-believe
people.

So I was stunned and unclear about how to respond when one day the kids in my neighborhood decided to sneak up behind me while I was playing in the driveway, pull open the back of my dress, and pour gravel, dirt, and mud down my back. They laughed with that ugly laughing sound made by people who are brought together by hurting someone else, the laughter that they hope will make them feel better about themselves. Startled and humiliated, I jumped up and began to cry. Darned if I didn't always just cry instead of turning around and giving them a piece of my mind or heart or something primal.

As I ran into the house, my mom glared out the window at the neighborhood that must have grieved her more than she ever let on and at the children of those families who taught them nothing about how to treat other people with kindness and courtesy. She took my dress off, then stood at the front door to shake out the rocks and dirt and "show them" how offended she was. Did anyone see this demonstrative act of disgust? I didn't know. I was still crying.

My precious mother looked at me and asked me the same question I was asking myself: "Why didn't you fight back?" I didn't know why. I just didn't.

Fast-forward to 1989, when I sat in the office of one of Nashville's top psychologists/marriage counselors. My husband and I had begun extensive marital counseling with David, and he was meeting with us both together and separately to discuss our potential for making our marriage and ourselves stronger and more whole. This was my first solo meeting with David, who my best friend Tori had nicknamed "Rambo Therapist." I was a bit nervous. The nickname fit him well, for he would oftentimes provoke me to anger or disgust or frustration just to move me into a place where I could verbalize why I believed what I did or why I reacted to situations based on my value system. He would find clever ways to jump-start places in my heart that were on hold…or fearful…or on ice.

On this particular day, David chose to end our discussion with an arm-wrestling match. At first, I laughed when he brought out a small table and asked me to arm-wrestle him. "You've got to be kidding," I said. He didn't smile back—that Rambo look was in his eyes. "No. Go for it." He put his elbow on the table and waited for me to move into position. "I can't wrestle you—you'll win!" I said. This was getting on my nerves. "Go ahead," he replied, his insistence never wavering.

After many more protests, I sighed, rolled my eyes, and put my skinny elbow down on the table next to his strong arm. Slam—it was over in a matter of seconds. "Of course you won!" I said with irritation. "This is stupid!" He looked at me calmly and said, "I didn't have to win." My agitation grew. "What in the world are you talking about? I'm not strong enough to beat you." Then he coolly replied in that this-is-why-I-make-the-big-bucks kind of way, "You didn't have to play fair."

It took a while for me to verbally wrestle through what he meant. But he meant this: I like to play fair. I had built my life on doing things fairly and honestly and the way I thought would be pleasing to God. David countered by saying that I could have beat him by standing up, using both arms, doing anything to shake up the status quo—fighting back without dishonoring my value system. Even Jesus stood up for what He believed in and used different ways of approaching unapproachable scenarios.

Somewhere in my subconscious I remembered my mother saying the same thing to me. "Sweetheart, why don't you just get mad and fight back?"

At the end of the session, David looked at me and said something he would repeat to me for years. "If there was one thing I could give you, one thing I could wish for you more than anything else, it's that you would have more fight."

More fight. How does a Christian like me use the word "fight" in her vocabulary? How do I know when to stand up and ask questions, or when to simply say "no" to a request? Aren't we supposed to die and die and continually die to ourselves? Doesn't that exclude fighting?

Over time and to this day, God has used many things to teach me that I have been given instincts for survival—instincts emotional, spiritual, and physical—that must be used to keep myself in balance. I have learned to fight for my children, and then to put their faces on mine when it's time to make a decision that requires the uncomfortableness of fighting back—of making a tough call...of confronting in love...of saying enough is enough. When I cannot find the fight in me, I have learned to say, "If this were Courtney or Graham, what would I want for them? What would I counsel them to do to represent themselves with integrity and godliness?" Somehow, putting their faces in place of mine makes things amazingly clear. In places where I would tend to feel unworthy to fight for myself, substituting my children's faces for my own clears the muddy waters.

I do believe it's possible and necessary to set boundaries for ourselves as Christians. Even Jesus left the crowds alone at times to "refuel," to pray, to have His own "down time." At times He must have left people who were begging for healing, people still in need of miracles. But He needed to go off and give Himself time to heal, time to gain strength for all that was required of Him on this earth. In spite of the countless miracles He performed, He still left this world with people dying of disease and desperate for His touch. *Even God on this earth couldn't be everywhere and everything for all people at all times.* It helps me to remember that Jesus had limits. Jesus had times when He felt sad, depressed, tired, and weary. And there were times when He had to fight for

His own heart to be renewed in the presence of His Father so He could come back to the forefront and be effective.

I once asked my pastor how he was able to deal with all the people around him who needed things from him. How could he possibly be there for everyone and talk endlessly to people like me who had questions with no answers this side of heaven—and still have enough time to be with his family and to just be quiet with God? He said to me, "Bonnie, you'll never be a truly effective minister for God until you learn how and when to say 'no.'"

Through my divorce I hit the place of fighting back. It wasn't until years later that I realized it was a form of fighting for my physical, emotional, and spiritual health. This was my weakness and my place of having to finally fight for the grace of God to move me on and to forgive me for my limitations. It was—and remains—so hard for me to admit that I was unable to make things all right in my first marriage. But I learned that I had limits. I learned that fighting for sanity and health can be as sacred a fight as one can face. Each person has a different wall of defense of his own humanness that requires fighting back, fighting for preservation of soul and body and for faith that can survive the fires of this world.

The concept of fighting for oneself can easily be misinterpreted in a world full of self-fulfillment rhetoric. That's neither my meaning nor my intention here. It's one thing to say, "I deserve this...so I will fight for my right to do this...." It's another thing to believe that Jesus never promised us the right to anything—except the right to depend on Him to walk with us through the pain of what is thrown our way or what we bring down upon our own heads. As believers in Christ, we do have a calling to know when to stand and face the demons in His name. And when we are unable to wrestle them to the ground, we must fight until the fight is out of us, then fall into His arms. But without the fight there is no awareness of our own inadequacy or, ironically, the dignity we bring to who God made us to be for this time and place and purpose. Fighting for ourselves requires humility, brokenness, and courage through Christ's blood.

Being a doormat in the name of Jesus never accomplishes much of anything. These "fights" that we learn to face as women and men of faith, we take on with much fear and trembling. Neither the wimp nor the steamroller will do. Jesus, our image-Maker, modeled for us the real deal. He fought for His personal peace with God, for the peace and wholeness of others, and left us with Paul the apostle's words: that we should run the good race, fight the fight, and reach for the prize, knowing all along that in the end, He has overcome and has won the final round.

Hope

~

Grace is an animal I did not understand. But a grace miracle still happened in spite of the droning minister of my childhood and the hell of Vacation Bible School summer after summer, for somehow the Word of God elbowed its way into my heart, stronger than the rest of the demons that fought for that space. I thank God for this, because as I traveled across the country like a clueless Doris Day—singing in clubs and trying to pursue my dreams in places I was not destined to be—truth kept me alive.

Nothing stings quite as sharply as betrayal by a close friend. Betrayals such as these blindside the hidden, trusting places in our hearts that want to believe the best about the people we love. Betrayals are cruel and selfish; they eat away at the one thing we all need at the end of the day—hope. And betrayal seemed to be out to rob me of my personal, professional, and spiritual confidence.

My musical group and ministry, First Call, began as a business venture between Marty McCall, Melodie Tunney, and me: a marketing of ourselves as a studio group in Nashville. We named ourselves after a phrase commonly used for the first musicians called by a producer for any given session. We also liked the idea of the title reflecting our common faith in Christ.

After years of being on the road in different situations, we'd each decided it was time to settle down, stay in one place, raise our young children, and have a more stable existence (if such a term could ever apply to a career in the arts).

I had written and performed in a comedy quartet called Ariel in the early '80s. Ariel had a strong local following in Nashville, and we had great enthusiasm for experimenting with comedy and video in live performance, in a way that our market had not seen before. This work is something I am still proud of, but our timing seemed misplaced, and ultimately Ariel seemed either ahead of its time or misaligned for whatever reasons.

Subsequently, I ended up singing more than acting, doing background vocal work on the road with Amy Grant and Russ Taff. Marty was breaking new ground in the rock scene—doing several albums and touring extensively with Fireworks. And Melodie had paid her road dues traveling with Truth and Michele Pillar. All of us were ready to settle down into the background studio scene and stay home.

Naively, optimistically, we worked hard to establish a niche for ourselves in the highly competitive studio singing industry, and we were thrilled when it wasn't long before we were singing every day in the studio on radio and television jingles, as well as for many top contemporary Christian music artists on their projects.

By the time Word Records executive Neal Joseph approached us to record an a cappella Christmas project, *Evening in December*, Sandi Patty had also begun to talk with us about accompanying her on her "Let There Be Praise" national tour. Reluctant to leave town again and certain we were not aspiring to be a recording act, we nevertheless entered both arenas, initially recording two albums of our own and singing on Sandi's tour—after which things began to snowball.

Throughout 1986 and 1987 we found ourselves singing with Sandi at the Grammy Awards, on *The Tonight Show,* and on tour in front of over 500,000 people. Our first several albums were nominated for Grammy and Dove awards, and we were as shocked as anyone when we won "Group of the Year" two years in a row.

None of us had envisioned this kind of acceptance and responsibility, and God graciously allowed us to grow into a deep embracing of this calling. At first I thought people just liked to listen to us sing because we sang so ridiculously loud! Over time we were amazed at how harmony can move and stir the hearts of so many people.

After our entry into the market as a recording act with Sandi, we recorded five albums over the next five years with Melodie, until she and her husband branched off to begin their own ministry. At this point Marabeth Jordan, a talented studio singer, joined the group. Marabeth's audition with Marty and me occurred during a background vocal session for a Rich Mullins album. She had no idea we were testing out our sound that day, and she seemed to blend vocally and personally with both of us in a thrilling new way.

Being in a group is much like being in a marriage. It demands compromise, sensitivity to each other's creative and spiritual hearts, and ongoing respect and space for each individual's contributions.

Marty and I had a choice about whether or not to hire Marabeth simply as a paid third singer or to make her an equal third member of the group. We opted to make her a full partner, wanting nothing to stand in the way of her giving her best energy and commitment to First Call's ministry.

Throughout all of our projects recorded as a trio, we would often discuss the miracle of how the Lord would take the songs we recorded in some dark, windowless studio and allow them to minister to His people. The greatest comfort any Christian artist can have is to know that God uses the music in spite of the musician.

And yet after many years of recording and working and riding the ups and downs of the music scene, First Call entered our tenth year of ministry not without our own fractured view of the industry at large and questions about our place in it. In the midst of this questioning, we embarked on the road with a highly coveted slot on the Michael English tour in the spring of 1994. Ironically, it was called the "Hope" tour. By the end of spring, it had been dubbed the "Hopeless" tour.

As the month of May rolled around, the affair that had begun between Michael English and Marabeth was out in the open. First Call lost its record deal and its ministry, and our friendships were racked with pain and anger. I could not avoid the obvious fact that betrayal was an issue I needed to confront.

Having already wrestled with this beast during my divorce, I had assumed that First Call was the one safe place it wouldn't rear its ugly head. How in the world did our ministry end up in such a maelstrom of tragedy?

Looking back at my journals, I can see a chronicle of warning signs and distress signals that started long before the tour. An erosion of purpose and unity had crept in over time—almost unnoticeable except in hindsight, where everything jumps into place with appalling clarity. The success machine mentality can easily sidetrack the purpose of any artist with promises that have little to do with eternal things. I believe this mentality began to creep in on us and keep us off balance. Distractions of solo career plans, money, and position also pulled us in different directions and warred against the true intentions of our hearts to serve God's work above all else.

How very much I felt that we had stopped asking questions about success and the price it could demand. On the "Hope" tour, ironies ran rampant. During the tour, First Call was in final negotiations with a huge label for signing the best and largest recording contract of our careers. We were out with Michael English—arguably one of the greatest talents our industry will ever know—on the hottest tour going. After ten years of seeking a stable place in an unstable industry, it all seemed to be coming together.

Yet I'll never forget the contrast between the moods on- and offstage every night. The tour was, creatively, a master-piece. Mercy Ministries' Nancy Alcorn brought a huge sense of meaning to each night with her riveting, compact presen-tation of the plight of unwed mothers and the hope her orga-nization brought them. Michael is a brilliant singer, and the band was full of some of the best players in Nashville. The sound was rocking, the production was awesome, and it was a powerhouse of a ticket. As for First Call, we were given what was quite possibly the best live performance opportu-nity of our career, and we sounded stronger than ever. The audiences were screaming, the tour was jammed, and onstage everything clicked. Yet offstage nothing flowed. No one knew quite how things were really unfolding. But to many people it was unmistakable that the situation was primed to explode.

The atmosphere of the tour seemed to spin out of control by the end of the spring—beyond any help that might have been offered or received. After the Dove Awards, when news broke of the affair and Marabeth's pregnancy, the last line said by the king at the funeral scene in Shakespeare's *Romeo and Juliet* rang through my head. After the lovers were found dead, after all the bigotries and protected agendas ended in tragedy, the king looked around and sadly proclaimed, "All are punished. All are punished." Beyond the hoopla of returned Dove awards, media cruelty, and trite sound bites, all of us were left lost in the silent rubble of stained min-istries, friendships, families, and an injured industry. All pun-ished.

Oddly enough, the night Marabeth called a meeting with Marty, me, and our manager to tell us she was pregnant with Michael's baby was the night I had planned on telling everyone I was going to leave First Call. That night is forever burned into my memory: Marabeth's pain, our shock, tears and prayers, and suddenly the solution to the mystery of the unspoken agony all around. This huge curtain fell away, and the pieces to the puzzle all came together. It was Marabeth, not me, who asked to leave that night.

Afterwards, driving home, I was a wreck. A tidal wave of anxiety and grief came over me. I couldn't breathe. I couldn't talk. I sobbed alone in my car and my insides felt like they were colliding. When I got home, my mom and dad were waiting with my children. The hardest thing was telling them what had happened. I couldn't hide the hysteria that fell on me with the intensity of all the months of suspecting something was terribly wrong and trying to push it aside. Graham, six years old at the time, ran up to his room to bring me forty-nine cents—his way of trying to secure my hope.

I guess you could say that my six-year-old, in all his innocence, mirrored the hope God would give me. Throughout the coming months of fear and the escalation of clinical depression, God kept me alive, little by little, forty-nine cents at a time—emotionally, physically, and spiritually. I began to pray like Christ suggested: "One day at a time...this day has more than enough to handle...just give me this day my daily manna of grace, Father."

Forty-nine cents. Almost fifty, but not quite. We're never quite there, but that's not our concern.

First Call continues to record and travel as a duo. It's different now, but the history we left is something that God still uses. The good we've accomplished for Him and the good we work at now have outweighed the pain of betrayals and the ways in which we've failed each other. I see Graham's forty-nine cents offered up to me every time someone comes to the record table at a concert, telling me how much they pray for us and play all of our music, thanking Marty and me for pushing on.

I went through the ugliest part of my life after the "Hope" tour ended, when depression threatened my faith to its core, but now I'm more certain than ever God is a God of great compassion and He does restore the years the locusts eat away. He restored my heart and soul, forty-nine cents at a time. I begged for the payoff, the fifty-cent mark, but He allowed me to hurt enough and become desperate enough to find His amazing grace. That grace has given me a new season of marriage and love that I don't deserve, but for which it has been His great pleasure to burn me through the fires and prepare me. Forty-nine little stinking, frustrating cents at a time...but still progress in the eternal scheme of things.

People of faith all hit the wall somewhere along the line. It just comes with our birth certificates, which should come with a postscript that reads: "Congratulations, welcome to the world! This note certifies that someday the rug will be pulled out from under you, so consider yourself fore-warned." Some walls fall down quickly and others crumble away little by little, but those walls are part of a fallen world. We lose jobs, friends, children, marriages, and dreams, and we hurt more than we think is possible. But God does not move. Even in the darkest place, He shows up in the face of a friend, a reassuring phone call, a smile from a stranger, or the six-year-old hand of a child offering all he has to bring to the moment. Like a lover who can't take "no" for an answer, our God is still there—coming in the Son, living and breathing and dying and living again so He can better under-stand the walls we face.

Hope. It's one of the big three—it accompanies faith and love—and at certain times, for me, the greatest of these is hope.

Conversation
with the Devil

~

Throughout junior and senior high school, I immersed myself in the arts. My schedule was filled with acting in community theater productions, playing flute and being a majorette in the marching band, performing in all the plays at school—and hanging out with anyone except a person who I could seriously allow into my heart. The males around me were mostly not interested in romantic relationships, and so I began to see myself as unappealing to the opposite sex. And although I was raised in a Christian atmosphere, I never seemed to see God's love for me as something relevant or accessible. By the time I entered college, I was convinced my calling in life was the arts and, most likely, I would never know the love and devotion of a man. It was something I desperately wanted, but somehow I thought I didn't deserve such a gift.

Looking back, I can see what distorted my view of myself as a woman created by God and loved by Him. My earthly father was a wonderful, gentle-hearted, tender man. But during my adolescence he stayed very distant from me, as was the custom of many fathers at this time. Now, as I watch Courtney growing up, I realize the critical role of a father in his daughter's life during this time of emerging womanhood.

I had boyfriends, but they were challenged by their own fragile search for manhood. And so I played easily into the role of being nonthreatening to and undemanding of them. We each supported the other's place of insecurity. The one man I became attached to in my late teens ended up embracing a homosexual lifestyle. To me this was a tremendous statement that I was not "woman enough" to hold his attention. I stuffed this pain down deep into a hidden place, not touching it for decades.

As I look back now at my 10-year marriage that disintegrated around me, I see how my own insecurity as a woman made my role precarious in that relationship. I assumed every problem was my fault. I was certain I was never *anything* enough for my husband. I tried to take on God's role, seeing myself as the one who would make or break our marriage.

Then, as a single and tremendously injured woman on the dating scene again, things got even worse. Those adolescent imprints, which were still there to haunt me, were compounded by the failure of my marriage. I had spent years in counseling, putting together the pieces of how a graceless theology led me to discount God's love for me. I wanted so much to allow His grace back into my heart and life. But as a woman with a distorted self-esteem—a woman left by her husband for someone else—deeper wounds than I could realize were scarring my soul.

Dating was one pitfall after another. I was confronted head-on with the rituals of the '90s dating scene, which basically consisted of making your own rules. I wanted to please God, please my children, *and* find love and redemption in the process. I met several precious men of God, and twice almost married in my eagerness for love and a restored family.

Through this all—after struggling with bouts of depression, crying out, and falling down and getting up again—this came to me: I needed first to seek after God. He and He alone was the One to woo me and teach me about my womanhood before I could be ready to find an earthly husband to share my heart and my life. After years of agony, I discovered His arms and His touch and His protection and quiet leading... and peace finally came.

Ironically, the lowest moment in my dating experience came after surviving two broken engagements. I had grieved about letting go of each of these men—men I had truly believed I was falling in love with. And I had begun to spend deep, alive time with God, thinking I was finally free and clear and at peace.

Then I met *him*. He was involved at the Christian school my children attended, and so of course I assumed he must be a Christian too. Even after a man who I'd dated admitted to me that the only reason he went to church was to hit on the women in the singles class, I still assumed if a man was in a church setting, he was safe.

Courtney was playing basketball for a Christian school, and I met this man at one of her games. I believed he was a godly man—he was at a Christian school, wasn't he? For a period of five to six weeks, he and I conversed while our daughters practiced and played. He was raising both his daughter and his son alone—their mother lived in another city—and I naively attached to his situation the purple heart of single fatherhood.

God tried to warn me, to prepare me—and I didn't listen. On a flight home from a concert—the night I would have my first and only "date" with this man—I was seated next to a kind Christian doctor. The Lord tried to speak a warning to me through this doctor, who shared with me about his faith and his marriage and how God sees us through anything. The doctor said that we needed to be careful, though. I told him about the man I was interested in and wondered whether a relationship with him might be the redemptive one I'd been praying for. The doctor said, "You don't even really know this man who you say you're opening up to. Be slow to let this unfold, and God will let you know what to do."

I remember thinking that the doctor, by profession, was most likely a cautious person. I was certain I had the correct read on the man I was interested in. And when I landed back in Nashville that night, I had a message from him inviting me to dinner. I was elated. This was the call I'd been waiting for.

The man's daughter and Courtney were going to be at a school/church winter camp that night and our sons were spending the night with friends. And so it seemed like the perfect evening for us to have our first date. Courtney, always excited to see me happy, helped me pick out a dress and jacket to wear. I called Tori at the last minute and asked her, "This sounds crazy, but what do I do if he wants to kiss me good-night? I mean, this is only our first date, but we've been talking for six weeks. I mean, I don't want to give the wrong impression. I feel so stupid! What would you do?" She laughed and replied, "Bonnie, you're not going to sleep with the man—you can kiss him good-night and he's not going to get the wrong idea!" We had a great girl talk and I promised to let her know how things went.

I was so sure this was going to be a magical night. God was in this. I just knew it.

I've gone over and over the mistakes I made that night, beating myself up time and again for each one of them. And I share them with you, hoping that they might stand as a warning if you're as predisposed to naivete as I am. First, I called the man and asked him whether I could meet him at the restaurant instead of having him drive to my house. But he insisted on coming to pick me up, saying he was "uncomfortable" with a woman having to drive to meet him. I thought he was being chivalrous. A true southern gentleman.

So I gave him directions to my house, and I waited. I cleaned up the den a bit, stoked a fire I had lit, poured a glass of wine for us to drink before we left for dinner, and waited some more. I imagined the two of us talking in depth about our children, our life interests, our processes of healing from divorce, and our faith.

My second mistake, after allowing him to come pick me up, was opening the front door when he rang the bell. I cannot fully describe in words the assault I suffered when he stepped into my front hallway. Never in my life had I ever felt under such an "attack." Because of the overwhelming physical and emotional tailspin that ensued, I was thrown completely off balance.

This man, without speaking, stepped into my house, grabbed me, and began to kiss me with such force that I was completely stunned. No one in all my life had ever treated me as a woman with such brutal disregard. Now, it might sound vaguely romantic to be "swept away," but let me be clear that this act was not in the least bit romantic or sweeping. This was an assault.

And my third—and biggest—mistake came as a result of my physical and emotional fear of this man. I'm a tall woman, but he towered over me, and he was tremendously strong. Worst of all, thinking we were friends and assuming he thought he was operating from a Christian perspective, *I tried to reason with him*. And so began my conversation with the devil. I laughed, shaking nervously, trying to make a joke, and the evening went from bad to worse to abusive.

Jesus too had a conversation with the devil. It happened at the onset of His public ministry after He had spent forty days fasting and praying in the wilderness. But Jesus knew better than to engage in any type of "reasoning" with the enemy. I would have done well to remember that He spoke the Word over and over again, calmly and clearly, with every attack. Jesus knew that the devil knew His most vulnerable points—physical hunger from being in the wilderness—and a deep desire to win the world. And Jesus was full of wisdom in putting forth the power and name of the Lord God—"As it is written..."—over and over until the devil finally threw up his hands in defeat.

In retrospect, I've wished many times I'd called a friend and had someone come remove this man from my house. Instead I kept thinking, *This isn't him! This isn't the man I've been talking with. I know that somewhere in there, I can find the real person and we can get through this in one piece.*

That night turned into a battle—with me begging to leave to go to dinner, with him trying over and over to get me into compromising physical positions. And he let loose his venomous anger toward the women in his past, which threw me off even more. I started to get scared and I cried, asking him to leave me alone, still thinking that every time he calmed down and backed off I'd "reached" him. Ever the missionary on the dating front, I tried everything I could think of to talk him into a sane place.

At one point, he sadly and tiredly said, "You're a Christian—I guess you must really believe what you say and sing about." Furious, I said, "What did you think I was like?" And, after hours of emotional struggle and me telling him again and again I was not going to bed with him, he left, saying "Well, it was worth a shot."

I shut the door, physically sore from the battle and, worse, disgusted that I had let such a sick man into my life and my home. I'd been in a rich season with the Lord, and then—boom!—this sharp blow to my heart and faith.

For days I cried, feeling deep shame and then anger. I went to my pastor and told him what had happened, and we prayed. Knowing my predisposition to beat myself up, he encouraged me to put this situation at the foot of the cross and to allow grace to once again start its work in me. But this was a hard process. Precious ground in my walk had been lost. And I had the tremendous desire to sue the man, who—ironically—was in the law profession. In fact, my comment that finally made him leave my house was, "You know, isn't this what people call attempted date rape?"

Women, please, please be careful. This man admitted to me that he loved to hit on women at sports functions at Christian schools. He admitted to me that his children were in the Christian school because the tuition was affordable, not because he wanted them to have the spiritual enrichment.

He admitted to me that he had intense anger toward women. If you're like me, a person with deep-seated tendencies to be a "pleaser" and to help people and make things all right, please realize this is a misplaced sense of ego. Only God can affect these places in men or women. I wish so much I had gotten a righteous anger going that night and had called the police. Many of my male friends said later, "Bonnie, why didn't you call me?" And I had to ask myself the same thing.

And this led me to one of the most painful realizations about myself as a single person of faith. All the faith in the world doesn't blot out or erase our need for human touch, for romance, for longings to be held and desired. In the final analysis, I realized the most stinging, humiliating reason why I kept trying to make the evening turn a corner. Somewhere in the assault and struggle, I must have still been somehow pathetically grateful to have a man finding me attractive and kissing me and holding me. And I am not really surprised about this. We are after all human, sexual people. God made us that way. But it is so important that we don't get ourselves into a situation where the water on dry ground is actually poison.

That night I was held, but I was hurt and treated like an animal. I was lucky to get out of it without being raped. God was merciful. Yet it still felt somewhat like I imagine rape must feel like. And date rape must be the most insidious kind of rape, because you are confused by the "friendship" you have with the person who is violating you.

So please be careful. Please be wise. Especially when you are filled with growing times with the Lord, because I believe the enemy strikes with appalling preciseness at our vulnerabilities. We must learn to do what Jesus did. He did not converse with the devil. He spoke the Word of God in all its blinding brilliance, and His words shut down the enemy.

Desperate for God

~

I was ripe for a breakdown by the time First Call left for the "Young Messiah" tour in 1994. Knowing absolutely nothing about clinical depression, I didn't recognize the symptoms I was experiencing, which were frightening—insomnia, crying, loss of appetite, caverns of despair into which I was swept by something like a dark, swift tide of black water. By the time the 12-city tour ended, I had barely eaten, and any sleep I'd gotten was limited to two-hour stretches.

When I returned home to Nashville, I went to see my pastor, Scotty Smith. Sobbing and unable to get a grip on my emotions, I told him how during the tour I would get myself together long enough to sing, then sit down and cry for the rest of the concert. The people around me were precious and dear—especially Max Lucado, Carman, Steve Green, Wayne Watson, and the 4 Him guys. Twila Paris prayed an especially moving prayer for me one night during devotions, as it was obvious that I was a basket case. They listened and tried to offer something to calm my tears, but by the end of the two weeks they could only offer hands of compassion on my shoulders.

Back in Nashville, even in the safety of my home, I was unable to pull myself out. I stood in grocery lines, quietly sobbing. I began to lose far too much weight and—more seriously—I began to lose my will to live. Knowing I would go to heaven someday, I began to fantasize about God taking me home as soon as possible.

My pastor, Scotty—the most amazing brother in Christ—prayed with me, then gave me wise counsel. First, he told me that I'd been barreling through a lot of loss and hadn't allowed myself time to fall apart. That time had now come. He told me to ask my closest friends to pray on my behalf, to picture lowering me through the roof of the house to Jesus, as the crippled man in the Bible was lowered. In my weakness, I could allow those who loved me to be strong.

Second—and this was wonderful advice to receive from a man I respect so much as a spiritual leader—he advised me to seek medical help. And so I spent many months getting professional help from doctors who taught me to take better care of myself physically and emotionally and who also prescribed drugs that allowed me to sleep again. I began to get stronger. And I reached out to people like I had never done before. I trusted them. I allowed them to hold me up in prayer.

Now, I'd like to be clear on something: As Christians, we take prescribed medication for physical illnesses with no sense of guilt. And when it is our emotions that are ill, we must also see medicine for our emotional illnesses with the same clearness of conscience. There are helpful tools that, if used with correct supervision and in balance, can greatly help those of us who suffer from chronic depression and insomnia. For me, this period of drug therapy brought me from a negative emotional balance back to ground zero. And until you're back at ground zero, there is no way you can have the energy to fight on—or even to pray.

Just as important, though, is the spiritual medicine one must seek during this time—the Word, good books and tapes, any reminder of God's faithfulness to heal soul as well as body.

During this time my friends and family held on to me with tenacious love and patience. Mom and dad drove carpool. Russ and Tori and Marty and Vickie all prayed for me, listened to me, and fed me. My sister and brother gave me money and time and books and their unconditional support.

Little by little, I fought back against the darkness. I read the Bible voraciously and also read from great writers like C.S. Lewis, Frederick Buechner, Max Lucado, Mike Mason, Philip Yancey, and others who wrote honestly about the disease of depression and the human condition of suffering.

Slowly I began to praise God in the dark. I had no choice but to move ahead, leaning on Him with my full weight, trusting Him to pull me out. My mother, alarmed at my condition, told me about my great-aunt Helen, who got in touch with me and shared with me about her own battle with clinical depression. I discovered that clinical depression had established itself in the lineage of the women in my family. She wrote me the following encouraging words: "Since my last bout with depression, and the Lord's walking me through that, I've had other trials. Some quite severe, and some that tested my faith at a deeper level. They have been tough, but now the bedrock is there, and the darkness did not return...a shade of gray perhaps...but when we have learned that God is good and will do us good, we can come to Him with open hands and a willing spirit."

I became a desperate woman. Or a woman desperate for God. As I came out of the depression, I began to see what a blessing my state of desperation had been. Falling apart completely and falling onto God has been the single greatest gift of my life. God taught me how strong His arms are. The Holy Spirit gently, consistently brought me to an understanding of my first and truest love. And Jesus has become my passion—knowing Him is the greatest, most interesting, and most compelling unfolding of my life.

Depression also motivated me to wrestle with God in a real way, something I had never before been brave enough or crazed enough to do. The idea of demanding a blessing from the Maker of the universe is ridiculously intimate. Even more staggering is God's passionate, affirmative response. All of us leave such an experience like Jacob did—forever changed, crippled yet redeemed, marked once again for life.

I learned that God loves me more than I can conceive of loving. He loved me enough to allow me to hurt dreadfully. He loved me enough to let me go for years with no answers to the questions and longings of my heart. He loved me enough to let me be disappointed, confused, and desperate. Just on the brink of giving up, I was shocked to discover the first few moments in my life when it felt like I was standing on holy ground. I found that in the very fabric of everydayness there was the miracle of the simple and the ordinary. Being at home, cooking a meal, singing a session, watching a ball game, doing nothing in particular at all—moments transformed into holiness.

Nothing is wasted.

Nothing is beyond redemption.

Blessed are the desperate.

Let the Healing Begin

~

Having recorded three additional projects as First Call—
the duo—Marty and I have had the blessing of being broken
and crushed and renewed by the events of the "betrayal"
years. The first single from our self-titled project is called
"Let the Healing Begin." We have sung that song in churches
that have been through their own losses—from being burned
to the ground and rebuilt, to losing pastors and members, to
surviving splits and rebirth. This song was written by Cheryl
Rogers and Lowell Alexander after the Oklahoma City
bombing. It was taken from a speech made by Billy Graham,
who said to the surviving families, "Let the healing begin
from this point forward." We believe that only in the arms
of Christ does true healing take root and change us.

A couple came up to me recently after we had sung "Let
the Healing Begin" in concert and shared their story. "Thank
you for starting the concert with the song about healing," the
man said. "My wife and I lost our first child at four weeks
of age. He died last week, and we just buried him. That song
has kept us going through the whole thing. We just play it
over and over. And we want you to meet our son with us
one day in heaven, when we can finally have his first birthday
party. Thank you for continuing to sing."

God truly does use crisis as an atmosphere for miracles.
Especially precious to me is the following passage Max
Lucado agreed to write and record, which now precedes "Let
the Healing Begin" in our concerts: "There's no distance too
great that God's love can't span it, there's no wound too deep

that God's kindness and grace can't heal it. So if you think you're too far, or your wound's too deep—think again, turn to Him, and let the healing begin."

And I love the following quote from Mike Mason's *The Gospel According to Job*, which quiets the unrest that betrayal began in me and that forgiveness through Christ answered: "The mind that is able to live with unanswerable questions, letting the roulette ball spin at will and yet still seeing the Lord's hand at work—this is the mind of true faith. This is the faith that can respond, whether in good luck or in bad."

I am learning to let the roulette ball spin and am discovering that I cannot control where it lands. All I can do is trust that wherever it lands, Jesus will be there with me. That's the only surefire thing in this world. And on certain, especially holy days, I can see extreme mercy in the path before me. Mercy and forgiveness beyond betrayal. Undeserved favor. My daily bread.

One
COLORS

Two
RED

Three
ORANGE

Four
YELLOW

Five
GREEN

Six
BLUE

Seven
PURPLE

Eight
RAINBOW

Often it is the ones who come apart at the seams who exhibit the greatest faith of all. Just to fall apart is nothing. But to fall apart at the hands of God is to lay down one's life for others. It is to show the world what it means to stand on a rock even when that rock feels like quicksand.

—Mike Mason, *The Gospel According to Job*

November, 1994

Clawing my way through this tunnel. I am crying out to God for removal from this process and I hear only silence. I feel under such a heavy cloud, and it feels like I come up for air and then go back under the water again.

December, 1994

(Upon deciding to break up with a man I intensely liked, as I knew the Lord was showing me that he and his ex-wife might reconcile.)

At some point I am sure this agony will turn too powerful to bear. Maybe if I'm lucky, I'll finally get bored with my own self-pity. This is the cutoff time, and I'd like to try to praise God in the middle of this for all He does to sustain me. It's a noble wish, to have a heart like Paul's that praises in the dungeon. I'm going to try.

December, 1994

Another day of despair. En route to St. Louis...this morning I had thoughts of death again, of how, if I didn't have my children, I might just long to be with God. Maybe what I'm saying is that I don't want to face what God is requiring of me here in this world. I just don't want to hurt anymore. His ways are not mine, but His ways seem so hard. When I think of all the men and women of the Bible called to a special walk with God, and what was asked of them, I want to scream, "I CANNOT HANDLE THIS! I CANNOT DO THIS! You're asking too much!"

December, 1994

I'm scared of myself today. My pain is at an all-time high. I don't think I've ever been this out of it. I lay on the floor last night, naked and crying and begging God to do something... another sleepless night.

January, 1995

Beginning to praise God for this experience. His love is severe but cleansing. I'm turning a hard corner somehow. Daily I confess my sins. I am slowly learning to forgive myself, to let myself off the hook, and, by doing so, not dishonoring what Christ did on the cross. I cannot lay my sins at His feet and continue to beat myself up with them. Let them go. Move on in grace.

February, 1995

There's a delirious kind of freedom feeling at this end of myself—this bungee jump into the arms of God....

Summer, 1995

Breathe, trust, pray, read, ponder, wonder, ask, and accept. Be, Bonnie, just learn to *be.* Be awake, but trust God to move and bring work and purpose in His mercy and time.

July, 1995

I feel like I'm wading into the waters of life again. Beginning to feel like maybe I won't go under. Let me never forget that I walk only in God's strength and His grace alone is my joy. There is no other place of contentment. Grace—and letting it flow in me to others—is medicine.

End of summer, 1995

God is moving me to a continued practice of forgiveness. I know that ultimately this is best, for it keeps my heart from bitterness, helps to heal the everpresent pain and rejection—to lean into the suffering of the cross and allow God to be undefinable. He giveth and He taketh away—yea, blessed be His name.

1995

Accusations that destroy are not from God.

September, 1995

Newest weapon against depression: At the first sign of reeling in my mind, I stop myself and list the things in my life I am grateful for. The top things I can remember as the highest points of my life:

1. Courtney's birth
2. Graham's birth
3. At age 11, winning the role of Alice in NAT's production of *Wonderland*
4. The first time I saw the water in the Caribbean with Russ and Tori
5. St. John
6. My first date with C
7. God's voice, on the tour in April, 1994: "Do not be afraid."
8. Ariel concerts
9. The day Graham won Best Athlete at basketball camp
10. Following Sting around at the Grammy party like a groupie
11. Maddie Rose saying "bah-bah" for Bonnie
12. The Rocky Mountains in August
13. Dancing in the cages at Ace of Clubs with Tori—GMA week, 1992
14. Being signed by Word in 1985
15. Being signed by Warner in 1995
16. The faces of people who are moved by the music we do
17. Being kissed by my children
18. Skiing in Pennsylvania
19. Winning my first Dove Award
20. All the Grammy nominations
21. Writing songs, especially "Broken Places"

1996

Losing things of great value allows great liberty—the great gift of the desert. This desert time gave me a chance to reexamine, refocus on my heart, career, desires, and relationships. It gave me a time to see what is and what is not eternal. Perspective. May I never forget what the desert gave me or what the wilderness burned into my heart...a great lesson of learning to walk in grace as daily manna to my body, this forgiveness of others, letting go of seeds of bitterness. May I ever be aware of whose name I carry over my work and heart and life like a stamp, an emblem, this name of my risen Christ. God, don't let me ever lose the memory of the desert, the mercy of the desert, and the deliverance from this desert.

1997

Sit at the feet of Job. There is much to be learned there.

Bridge Child

~

The cross that held Jesus' body, naked and all
marked with scars, exposed all the violence and injustice
of this world. At once, the Cross revealed what kind of
world we have and what kind of God we have:
a world of gross unfairness, a God of sacrificial love.

—PHILIP YANCEY, *Disappointment with God*

I was the bridge child between my mother and my grandmother. My mother gave of herself to my brother, sister, and me in all the things she so very much needed, the things she never received from her own mother. Born during the Depression, mom was the firstborn daughter of three children to a wonderful, God-fearing couple. My grandmother, Bonde Louise, was a forceful woman of her own, one of nine siblings and proud of her heritage. Her father was a prominent preacher in North Carolina, and my grandmother carried on the tradition of "preaching" with great passion. Her husband—my grandfather—was a gentle-hearted, quiet type who both respected and feared my grandmother's volatile qualities. They raised three children—two daughters and a son—to love God and others in a world full of turmoil and war. My mother knew the devotion and love of her father, but her mother, for unknown reasons, was never able to reach out to mom and give her the deep devotion a child needs to hold on to.

When I was born, I was given the name my grandmother went by—Bonnie. It seems I was offered up as a "look what I did for you" prize from my mom to her mom, both as an honor and as a request for affection. My grandmother loved me dearly and never failed to let me know of her devotion. Yet she went to her grave without showing this same affection to my mom. Consequently, my precious mother has spent her life making sure her three children never doubted for a moment where her heart stood.

My grandparents' marriage was a strange combination of love, devotion, and tremendous imbalance. My grandfather—"Papa"—was from the other side of the tracks. His family lineage was simple and mundane, and Grann constantly spoke of how "blessed" he was to have married someone of her background. The way in which she openly disregarded his people seemed amazingly bold and somewhat offensive to me. But no one around me questioned her comments, so I filed them away somewhere in my mind as just the way she was.

In many ways, my mother carried on this pattern in her own way. Feeling as if she needed to shield my father from some of the realities of our lives, she would make comments like, "Your dad shouldn't know this—he just couldn't take it." Somehow she thought that dad would crack into a million pieces over things that my mom felt she could absorb. I wonder if this image of mom taking care of dad, and Grann rescuing Papa from his family—this message that perhaps women are stronger and more capable than men—did not serve me well in my adult romantic relationships.

Ultimately, by the time of my divorce, I found that I could barely take care of myself and had done a disservice to my ex-husband by trying to take care of him for most of our marriage. And our marriage, of course, went the way of so many marriages in this decade—another statistic in the "dissolutions of marriage" section of the local newspaper.

After the divorce, stumbling through the wreckage of all the elements that brought Daniel and me to the point of separation, including his love for another woman, I realized I had to spend some serious time with God seeking His definition of womanhood. I realized during months of counseling that, among other things, coming to terms with my own roles in the marriage was an eye-opener. Indeed, I had taken over far too many responsibilities in the marriage and been the third—possibly fourth—generation of women in my family who had "taken care of the men." There were issues on both sides, but as hard as I knew I had tried to change and let go of behaviors and learn to love my husband better, I had failed. Or at least it felt that way, because his heart went to another. Overall, I realized I was a pretty wretched woman.

But the strangest, most wonderful thing happened to me through peeling back the layers of my humanity and finding out what a mess I was. As I studied the life of Christ, I noticed that He chose to spend His time reaching out to wretched women! Suddenly, feeling like the poster child for failure didn't seem quite so disgraceful. Jesus seemed to take particular pleasure in turning around the lives of the most ridiculously appalling women He could find. This was good company to be in, I decided.

I prayed, begged, and pleaded with God to teach me what He must have longed for Eve to know in the garden. What was it to be fully woman in His eyes? How would it be to be fully woman as a wife? As a mother? As a friend? I wanted to amend the legacy of strong women in my family by showing my daughter that strength did not always mean taking care of situations or finances or things that can be shared by a mate. Men have their obvious strengths, and women should be able to celebrate theirs. I was on a mission to revise and live out what it meant to be fully female as *God* defined femininity, not as the world had programmed me to believe. And where would He allow me to flourish, even after the divorce and the landmines I'd fallen onto during dating? Was it possible for me to fall far enough from the tree I came from to make my life different...and to make my children's view of marriage and womanhood different as well?

Over time—years, thank you—this blonde head has slowly awakened to one change at a time. It's taken a while, but I'm discovering this whole new concept of having the choice to say "no" to certain areas, to stop playing like I'm Superwoman. And eventually, after I'd gotten through the first few courses, God did bring Brent into my life.

I must say that even now it all continues to boil down to one thing: God's grace. His grace alone covers me and keeps me following the paths that I question with my new husband, my children, my career and calling...with what calls me as opposed to what drives me. His grace is the thing. Alone. Without starting there, nothing else evolves. And with that grace, the seeking begins to make sense here and there— more often now than not.

I believe God made woman to be in wonderful, joyous, painful, growing, intimate, passionate, and precious relationship with one man. First, as a woman I have to let God love me. And I have to find His arms before I can allow my husband's arms to hold me or his love to touch my heart. But by following God's plan—submission—giving over becomes receiving. And letting my husband lead grows into respect that breeds tremendous longing and affection. And all the girl-stuff I bring to the table stands out like jewels— as God intended. In fact, some days I think He made woman second because He saved the best for last!

Suffering

~

Cindy Carlson, one of the greatest single moms I was ever privileged to meet—truly a prototype of how to do this single parent thing and stay godly, sane, and even joyful—went to be with God in the summer of 1997. She left behind her a legacy of courage, hope, and love to her two teenage sons.

To others of us—like me, people on the outer fringes of her life—Cindy left an example of how to suffer well and how even to use the suffering as a platform for celebration.

Cindy fought cancer for years and was besieged with battles both emotional and physical. But her life spoke of abundance in the smiles and laughter that never left her. It was uncanny how this woman, vital and alive and just so very real, was able to give of herself to everyone around her with an effortless kind of elegance. She sat at the front desk of the school my children attended, and she was the first person people saw when they walked into the school. This school had its own cross of opulence to bear, and what could have been an intimidating entrance for a visitor or newcomer was made simple and down-to-earth because of Cindy's personality.

Did the kids she loved every day know she was suffering? Only a few very close friends knew of her bouts of pain with the cancer, the treatments, the emotional roller coaster of "now it's gone, now it's back." Yet this awesome woman handled the single-parenting of two sons for over a decade while battling cancer—without being a burden to anyone.

She sounds like a saint.

She wasn't. That's what I adored about her.

Cindy walked up to me the first day I was on spring break in Florida with the kids from the school. A huge gathering of people from the school and church were having a service the first Sunday we were there, singing and relaxing by the water. I didn't know that many people there, and I felt very much out of place. I was one of the only single moms I knew of, and everywhere I looked there were couples.

Well, Cindy just came over to me with this huge smile, held out her hand, and said, "Bonnie! I'm so glad you are here! Tomorrow night is the traditional 'single mothers' dinner out night' and you have to come! We go out and have a blast—no kids allowed. Please tell me you'll come." I was amazed by her knowledge of my personal situation and that somehow she and the other single moms had started a partying tradition years earlier. I felt lucky to be included.

You bet I went out to dinner with my comrades the next night. There were only five of us, and off we went, all dressed up and ready to go to the most expensive place we could find—a place that rarely allowed children to darken its doors! We ate seafood and salads and drank fine wine and talked and laughed over the course of the evening, the walls around our hearts sweetly melting. We shared stories about ex-husbands and money and heartache and the question of whether or not to ever again entertain the notion of dating and maybe chancing a dance with love. It was the best kind of girl-talk.

Cindy was free-rolling and fun and full of jokes. She was human, fully woman, fully alive in every sense of those words—open to love again, open to life, open to what the next day might bring, and not really concerned about much else. Most of the other women there had known Cindy for a long time and had seen her through the ugliness of her divorce and the seasons of cancer she'd endured along with the stress of raising two sons.

What I didn't know at the time was that she had just been through another diagnosis, which pointed toward more chemotherapy. Looking at her beauty that spring night in Florida, it would have been impossible to guess that she would be gone by the summer. She radiated survival.

At her funeral, there were tears, but they were all mushed together—tears of joy, tears of celebration, tears of missing her, tears for her sons' loss. We laughed, we cried, and as Ashley Cleveland sang "Amazing Grace," I could feel Cindy looking down at us all, shouting and laughing and just knowing how she was loved. Most likely she'd have been a bit embarrassed by the packed-out church building that held around two thousand people. She'd have loved how her mom spoke so beautifully about her life—her mom who died of cancer the next year.

But Scotty, our pastor, put into words a phrase I will never forget, which translated itself within my heart like this: "Cindy, *suffering was your pulpit.* From your pain, everyone tasted your faith. Defeat did not win out. Death did not have the last word, for even as cancer stole your physical body from us, your life shouted, 'No!' You did not lie down and roll over. You did not become bitter or desolate. Instead, you seemed to embrace the suffering, and through it your cross seemed to grow lighter. It almost seemed like you bore ours with your own."

Suffering was your platform.

Suffering was your love song to the Lord.

Suffering was your triumph.

What We Know

~

There is so much we weren't supposed to know.

We were children in a garden, walking in the shadow of our Father who was and is and is to come—He who is able to deal with both good and evil and everything in between.

We were made after His good.

We were not gods ourselves, but we were made after His likeness. With one exception. *We were not made to understand evil.*

Yet we tried to reach out for more and were bitten in the process—infected with the venom of an energy of destruction that has been a cancer ever since.

Don't eat of the tree, because the tree is full of fruit that only God can handle. God wrestles the devil down and fights battles we cannot understand. Humans fail miserably in this venue, this drama. God has been rescuing us ever since we barreled into scenes we weren't written into.

We were made to love and laugh and enjoy good things, like children innocent of the potential to destroy those very things made for our pleasure. Things like food, sex, love, nature, intimacy, and possession.

God found a way to restore us to a childlike place with Him again by giving Himself back to us. But the result of wanting what we aren't equipped to handle is that a world which wasn't made for destruction is now in the process of being destroyed.

Emotionally, physically, and spiritually, we weren't made for rape, for disease, for injustice, for torment, for prejudice, for divorce, for single parenting, for depression. Yet God the Father is able to deal with it. He walks beside us, bowing His head in pain with us, wishing that the gift of free will hadn't backfired on us. Yet He is unwilling to let us go, unwilling to let what we cannot handle eat us alive. He dies the deaths, cries the tears, and is patient, knowing that beyond this misunderstanding lies more. The cross will bear us over and into that next place—in His mercy, by His grace, we are not lost in the act of trying to be what we cannot be. We bow, falling to our knees in gratitude that God did not leave us, grateful that He loves us with an everlasting love, even though we are as rebellious and silly and stubborn as preteens who can't drive the car but insist on getting behind the wheel.

Praise to the unspeakable name of Him who created this world and still loves it in spite of what it has become! Through the unspeakable price of the blood of His heart, His Son, and in His name, Christ: *Alleluia.*

Foot Washing

~

It took one year for me to completely hit the wall within my heart and soul. I say one year, but looking back, I think I had been storing up for a doozy of a breakdown for about five years. I barreled through being a single parent and aced the test of getting further and further into debt year by year. I barreled through the treacherous terrain of dating again. And I barreled on through what Marty and I had to face—we finished out what concerts were left, the ones that weren't canceled, with another mega-talented studio singer, Lisa Cochran. She graciously filled in for Marabeth and went on the road with us to finish up the "Young Messiah" tour we were contractually bound to complete in December. I was reeling in pain and didn't know what to do with it all.

My marriage had come apart over the same issues that now fractured my career and ministry. The question of what to do with the feelings of anger, outrage, injustice, and guilt bombarding me, and questions about my own responsibilities weakened me over the months.

During this time, I also began to date someone who I believed I could fall in love with, who might be the answer to my prayers for remarriage and happiness, only to find that he was still dealing with feelings for his ex-wife. I felt the Lord directing me to exit this man's life, and I didn't want to. But I knew I had no choice. This was not God's man for my life, for my future—no matter how badly I wanted to shoe-horn him into that role. As I felt more and more loss building in my heart, the hopelessness descended. And it seemed that betrayal and heartache were all I faced every day. A crack started to slowly, steadily widen—everything was tearing away at me like the iceberg tore open the *Titanic*—and I began to sink. And so the stage was set for my breakdown on the "Young Messiah" tour.

On the first day of rehearsal this wonderful man, Max Lucado, walked up to me, looking a bit puzzled. "Haven't we worked together somehow, somewhere before?" he said, then paused. "Did you by any chance go to Abilene Christian University?" Both of us laughed as we remembered. I had been at ACU for one semester, and he and I were in the same class, where I ended up being a choreographer for an a cappella showcase we sang in.

Suddenly I could recall this tall, redheaded guy dancing away in the back row of a group of one hundred sophomores, and I knew that God had sent me a special counselor for this tour. Max held Bible studies for us each day, and I ended up weeping and asking him to help me many times during that tour.

After the tour, Max's teaching on forgiveness was the lifeline that I grabbed on to, which began a process of healing for me. He sent me a tape of his wonderful rendition of the lessons to be learned from the story of Jesus' washing the feet of His disciples.

Through Max's words, I began to see this story beyond the Bible school stereotypes. It struck me hard that if the perfect Son of God could get down on His knees, take a tub of water, and in humility and love wash the dirt and grunge off *all* the feet around His table—even the feet of the ones who would deny and betray Him—then what possible right did I have to hold anything against anyone who had betrayed me? How much of my oncoming depression had to do with the unforgiveness I still held toward my ex-husband, Marabeth, and anyone else who had hurt me? I began to face the hardest questions of my life during this inventory of my own heart. But this process began to free me to forgive—to forgive even myself.

With a huge sense of my own unworthiness, I began to look at things through the filter of forgiveness. I had not learned to forgive anyone, including myself, for the failures surrounding me. It was time to live in a daily, ongoing awareness of how much forgiveness had been extended over my life, allowing me no right whatsoever not to work hard to extend the same spirit of grace over those who had hurt me.

The following passage in John revealed even more: that those I forgive are then released to be forgiven in the eternal world: "[Now having received the Holy Spirit, and being led and directed by Him] if you forgive the sins of anyone, they are forgiven; if you retain the sins of anyone, they are retained."

Evidently, if I held on to the pain of unforgiveness, there was a serious question as to whether I was also holding others in this prison of pain as well. So I began to let go and to embrace and receive the grace of forgiveness. I have to admit, the kicker in it all was to taste the intense relief and healing that came with cleaning off these dusty feet I had in my mind, feet that had been sitting at my table for years. I began to visualize the humility of Christ on the cross, Christ at the well with the woman living in sin, Christ healing, touching, and loving me in my most sickening places of despair. After a while, I began to crave forgiveness, for I discovered that forgiveness is the best medicine for a bad case of betrayal.

I believe there should be little energy for unforgiveness in our lives as believers. What purpose does it serve? Does it right the wrongs? Does it justify our own self-righteousness? Does it do any good at all?

Truly, in betrayal and sin all are punished. Yet beyond that, Christ endured the ultimate punishment for all betrayals large and small, and that's the end of the story.

Nothing else is needed, and nothing else really holds water. The enemy betrays. The enemy inspires betrayal in the most hurtful ways. Yet there is peace beyond betrayal in forgiveness, for God never leaves us where the enemy takes us. His love is evermore faithful to find us in that place of pain and loss and to move us on—if we will let Him.

Most days now, all it takes for me to forgive is a long, honest look in the mirror—and one long, long look into His face.

Sisters

~

Amy, it's your big sister—hey, First Call is singing at Estes Park in a few weeks in Colorado—it's hot as snot—let's go together and drive around the mountains for a few days—can you possibly get away?"

What did we do before voice mail? My sister Amy and I have this amazing ongoing friendship/accountability/encouragement thing going on almost solely through our voice mail. She is many years younger and many years wiser than me, and I adore her. This is the little girl I played with like a toy when she was little and yelled at for wearing my clothes when we were older—and now she's one of my closest friends. She is a flight attendant for American Airlines and also does a mean real estate business on the side.

Amy and I also have shared the deep dream of marriage and family. We cried and prayed and laughed together, and checked out the possibilities for each other with a sense of humor and faith that remains a bedrock of comfort in my life. We'd been trying to get away on a short trip together for months, and so this year—my tenth year of singing at the Estes Park seminar in the Rockies—I finally got my baby sister to go along with me. We had a blast in spite of our "blonde handicap," which left us happily lost most of the time.

First Call was invited to fill an unexpected slot for an artist who could not attend, and we had a powerful time watching how the Lord, to our amazement, continues to speak a message of healing through our music. After all the times I'd sung there, from singing background vocals for Amy Grant, Russ Taff, and Sandi Patty to several First Call appearances, I'd never felt the Holy Spirit move more strongly than I did that night when we sang "Let the Healing Begin." It was doubly fun because Amy was there and I could share it with her—lost luggage and all!

After I completed my commitments at Estes, Amy and I took off and drove over the Rockies in our rental car through an intense fog, terrified both by the wonder of the mountains and the challenge of being able to see only inches in front of us as we traveled over the Continental Divide and into Vail. God granted us safety and a fabulous hotel room, which we were thrilled to find. We set off to wander aimlessly through the shops, looking at all the things we could never afford and just reveling in the beauty of God's handiwork in that gorgeous place.

In Vail, we both wanted to ride the gondola to the top of the peaks and had to wait an hour for the last trip to leave. No one was on the ride but Amy and me, and we just went wild talking about everything on our minds. Mostly we just had a great time being girls—sisters—together. That summer we were sharing our dreams of marriage and men, dissecting each other's dating lives and futures. During my single-again years, it was entertaining and it also felt good to be around another woman—especially my sister—who longed for a mate as much as I did. But there would always come the moment when we'd stop laughing and joking and would sit down and pray that God would hear the cries of our hearts.

Amy and I were the last people off the mountain that day in July. Riding the gondola down, we were overcome by the staggering beauty and power of the mountains all around us. It was dusk, and rays of light were just beginning to color the clouds around us. The mountains seemed to cry out, "We were made before you drew breath and will be here until the end of time. In our magnificence, see the strength of the Lord God Almighty! He is *I Am*!"

Without intending to, I began to pray. It was like the mountains commanded me to. Amy and I held each other's hands and prayed to God like little children: "Lord, hear our prayers for husbands. Hear our heart's desires and make us ready for the men You would have us to be with. Give us, please, the courage to believe that You will do Your perfect will with these dreams, but please, please keep our faith strong and our love pure."

Suddenly, Amy looked up and gasped, "Bonnie—look at the rainbow! It's for us—there's no one else here!"

There to the right of the car, in the middle of the mountains with no rain falling, was the most glorious, beautiful rainbow. There was no one in any of the cars traveling up and down the mountain, and we were silent in the moment. I fell to the floor of the car, weeping.

We cried now, praising God and thanking Him for saying to us through this rainbow, "I remember. I hear you. I know you. I am here." All the way down the mountain we cried and prayed and reached out together to love our Father who loved His daughters so much that He gave us a moment of His glory to hold on to.

At the bottom of the mountain we could hardly wait to rush off the car to find our rainbow. We looked up and searched to find it, but it was nowhere to be seen. You could only see it while in the air. Ever since then, Amy and I have seen rainbows together several times on clear and sunny days, for no reason whatsoever. Call us crazy—or desperate; I choose to believe that we were being loved by our Father and encouraged not to give up. It has been a hard road for both of us not to give up at times, feeling we truly don't deserve these signs of God's love and that maybe our dreams would never be fully realized.

Amy has teased me about this experience since then, saying that I fell to the floor and prayed like Mary, who wiped Jesus' feet with her hair, while Amy sat there quietly watching like Martha, who stayed in the kitchen.

Truth be told, Amy has the strongest faith around and often keeps me on my knees with her stories of God's grace covering her through her airline travel and her own journeys through love and life.

More than anything, these rainbows helped both of us to remember God's faithfulness. Since I might have forgotten the first experience, it seems that God made sure we saw rainbow after rainbow during that next year. And most of the time, Amy and I were together when we saw them, usually on a perfectly clear day. If I tended to forget the signs of God's promises and started to complain about my loveless life, Amy would just smile at me and say, "Bonnie, remember the rainbow."

One
COLORS

Two
RED

Three
ORANGE

Four
YELLOW

Five
GREEN

Six
BLUE

Seven
PURPLE

Eight
RAINBOW

We are alive when instead of killing time, we take time. We are really alive when we listen to each other, to the silences as well as to the words....We are really alive when we love each other...taking time enough to love our little piece of time without forgetting that we live also beyond time.

—Frederick Buechner, *The Hungering Dark*

"The Present"

Recognize the Present
Although it's not always pleasant
For if you turn your back
Stability you will lack
For the Present is not always a choice
It's here and it has a voice
The Present you have to face
The Present you have to embrace
Through all of the suffering and all of the pain
A stronger heart is what you will gain
You will find your courage from heaven above
You will learn to live and to love in the Present.

—Courtney Keen

1990

Courtney cried a little when I told her she was going to her father's house tomorrow night. She looks heavy-hearted. I asked if she wanted to talk about it and she just said she loved being at home.

August, 1990

Humbling, hilarious moment this morning. Courtney looked up at me from those blonde curls and said, "Mamma, you always say 'THIS IS THE RULE OF THE HOUSE' and then you break it!" I had to laugh at her incredibly honest and accurate assessment of my flaky attempts at single parenting.

Late summer, 1990

Courtney broke my heart last night. After her father left, she asked me, "Is daddy happy? I hope so. Is he coming back home with us? When can he move back in? You said you'd never get a divorce." I tried to explain that some things happened that I never anticipated. She teared up a little and said her life was hard, and asked me why life is hard.

I tried to be brave and told her God was still watching over us.

1990

Courtney had a tummy virus last night—high fever. I was up all night with her. Alone and nervous...I'm such a scared little girl inside. When I see the night falling, and I know I have to be mommy and daddy, I get so scared.

1991

I think Graham has seen *Pinocchio* a few too many times. He looked at me today and said, "If I sat on a fire, I wouldn't be real anymore."

1991

Graham asked me today, "Why do you call me and Courtney your bunny-heads?" I told him that bunnies were my favorite animal. He said quite clearly, "But I am a human." I stand corrected.

1992

Courtney came in tonight and asked me to pray the prayer to accept Jesus into her heart. On our knees, my sweet daughter and I prayed. And Courtney gave her life to Christ. What a gift! A miracle! I felt God's hand once again surrounding my child—and me—and Him saying, "I AM. I AM HERE. SHE IS IN MY CARE."

1992

All of my energies are going into trying to get my finances in order, to keep the house healthy for the kids and me, and to somehow just be a mom. When I see how much Courtney and Graham need me here, how much I need to give to them, I wonder what kind of mother I would be if there were a man in my life right now.

1993

My children fill me up with purpose and laughter and striving for all that is beautiful and strong and proud here. I come home to this sweet house that God has allowed us to keep, and I know finances are bad, but God continues to provide. Somehow I make ends meet. Courtney is so very lovely and Graham is so tender—my woman- and man-children. He's playing t-ball and she's having t-parties, and life is, at moments, very holy.

1993

Graham is delightful. He informed Courtney and me that he "broke up with his love last week." (Referring to Sarah at preschool—he wrote "Anna—not my girlfriend" on his right foot and "Sarah is my girlfriend" on his left foot. Somewhere the left foot lost out too.) He waters the dogwood trees for me and tells me, "I'm giving them a drink, Momma—they are so thirsty!" Courtney, my bright star, is so bored if she's not occupied at all times. From birth she's sought stimulation—so creative—so it's no surprise to me that she and Christa won three of the four possible awards at acting camp for creativity, performance, and teamwork. She is hurting right now, still full of confusion about the divorce. Last night she cried a little all through dinner and asked me if it would hurt this bad all summer. Her father is getting married next weekend.

1993

Courtney, commenting on her aging "bankie": "I loved the yellow right out of it!"

Graham, right before he threw up: "Come out, come out, wherever you are!"

End of Year, 1993

Courtney asked for a phone for Christmas. I'm having fun watching her grow up. Had to beg for her to make Santa pictures...at the mall with her brother. Reluctantly, she gave in. Graham has named and given ages to all of his fingers. It's hilarious. We are on our way to Washington, D.C. for a getaway with my new friend, Dale Hansen Bourke. We had a great Christmas. The kids give me purpose.

1994

Graham loves it when I am home in my terry-cloth bathrobe. He sighs and says he loves the smell, and says, "Mommy's home."

1994

I took Graham, who just turned six years old, on the road. When Mark Lowry asked why my son is so cute, Graham answered, "Because I don't smoke." When Veronica came over to sit with us at dinner Graham said, "You're lucky, you get to eat supper next to my mommy." And when he woke up the morning of his sixth birthday, he jumped up and said, "I'm taller! I grew overnight!"

November, 1994

Called home and Graham had left the following message on the machine: "Hi, Mommy, this is Graham. I just wanted you to know there's a tornado watch for middle Tennessee. Don't be scared and whatever you do, don't cry. But I just wondered what you'd say….Hugs and kisses, xoxoxoxo! I love you!" Don't be scared that there's a tornado watch and I'm in another state?!

December, 1994

The last two days have been a whirlwind of "doing." Yesterday the angels must have worked overtime keeping me going. After getting home on two flights, having left that morning at 4:00 on my body's time clock, I drove to the grocery, to Franklin to get the kids, home (napped for two hours—smartest move I made), then woke through some kind of unbelievable willpower. The kids and I took down the Christmas stuff, repacked it all, and put it away. Then I did laundry, dinner (on the grill), dishes, paid the bills, balanced the checkbook, unpacked, and prepared to repack—then vacuumed the house and got to bed by 11!

January, 1995

Courtney is really starting to look more and more like a little lady. Last night, she informed me that she wanted to change all the wallpaper and artwork in her room and pack away the baby dolls and Barbies! I don't think I'm ready for this. She and I giggle and laugh and talk a lot. She goes through my clothes and takes out things to wear. She's writing poetry, amazing and insightful, loves sports, and she and her friends talk on the phone all the time now.

August, 1994

The kids pooled all of their money and bought me a 30-dollar gift certificate to my favorite store in Franklin. I don't know if I can ever spend it—it seems such a treasure.

1994

Graham says there is a "babe" at soccer camp. She has long blonde hair and a pretty face, long legs and arms, and he cannot wait to wear his new Umbros because all the girls will love him.

March, 1995

Graham came in after his bath and pronounced, "Mommy, tonight in the tub, I made my first fake burp! I love special occasions!" Aah...the joys of manhood.

Summer, 1995

Courtney, Graham, and I are having an incredible time on our first real vacation! I am convinced the Lord moved me to do this on faith because it's been so healing, refueling, fun, and bonding! Courtney keeps telling me how much she loves me. Sunday night she said she was glad I was strong and brave enough to take us on this trip. No matter what happens in the future, I will always be grateful for this "eternal time" with my children.

1995

I have Court and Graham's best friends over to spend the night. They are awesome kids, but the noise level stresses me out so much—had to put in earplugs!

August, 1995

My sweet babies stayed home and we rented movies and ate lots of food! Watched *The Brady Bunch* and howled—then afterwards, Courtney told me she wanted to be an actress like me. The same desire to be in the arts is in her, and it's strong. I want to say "No! Have a life!" yet such rich parts of my life have been in connection with the arts. I just want Courtney and Graham to have some stability.

Fall, 1995

Courtney came into my room last Saturday morning and said, "Mom, I don't have any Umbros to wear to basketball!" Then she looked down at my gray flannel boxers and smiled. I said, "Okay—wear these." A few moments later, she said, "Mom! I have no sweatshirt to wear!" and smiled again at my gray sweatshirt. We both died laughing as I handed it over— something tells me I'm looking at lots of closet robbery in my near future.

1996

Wisdom from Graham:

"Meekness is not dorky, flimsy, or weak. If you're meek, you are humble and you will forgive people and ask them to forgive you.

"If you're too proud to say you're sorry, it's like you've built up too much milk or juice or water and your water is filled up and about to spill out. You should keep your pride low so it won't ever fill up too much.

"Grace is like when you're on this ladder and you do a good thing and you go up the ladder a little bit and then you do a bad thing and down you go a little bit...but in the end, no matter where you are, Jesus will always lean down from the top of the ladder and pull you all the way up!"

1996

Note: Decorating the house for Christmas this year, for the first time ever that I can recall, was a peace-filled thing. No arguments, no "me having to do it all just right." Courtney guided Graham through decorating the tree—it looks more beautiful than ever. Graham and I did the Snow Village and Nativity scene, and I just let the rest come together a little at a time. The house looks like a dream.

1997

Destin, Florida—spring break with the kids…more of a break for them than for me, but that's what it's all about. I am not at peace. Still wrestling with the repercussions from my hell date.

1997

Courtney is so beautiful and elegant and smart. I am completely proud of her. I am also acutely aware of the places she now goes in her budding womanhood, places that I must respect and leave her alone in. It is for her to find. It's a bittersweet thing to watch, full of joy and sorrow.

"Give Them Wings to Fly"

There will be broken dreams that I cannot repair,
Silent tears my hands will never dry
But far beyond the reaches of my love
I know You will be there
Father, hear their every cry
And give them wings to fly.

—Bonnie Keen and Scott Brasher, from "Give Them Wings to Fly"

Crazy Grace

~

They that wait upon the LORD shall renew their strength;
they shall mount up with wings as eagles; they shall run
and not be weary; and they shall walk and not faint.
—ISAIAH 40:31 KJV

Deep thoughts by Mommie Dearie," says my 16-year-old daughter when she doesn't want to hear me speak about serious sentimental issues anymore. When she's tired of what I'm saying, she calmly states, "Thank you so very much, and this now concludes 'Deep Thoughts by Mommie Dearie.'" Her frank words often hang over my head when I'm writing. She's not always around to say them, but her editorial sensibilities have a way of following me wherever I go. And a way of making me smile. And this is my book—so I can share all the deep thoughts I want!

Courtney Bonde Keen was born on October 11, 1983, brought into this world by a golf-obsessed doctor who wanted me to get on with the birth so he could make his afternoon tee time. Without going too much into the gory details, the doctor basically grew impatient with my pushing—and with the forceps—and pulled her out of my body with such force that I prayed out loud for God to protect my baby from the brutal process. The doctor broke Courtney's collarbone in the delivery, something that nobody knew for weeks. She cried and was in pain for three weeks before we discovered the problem. I should have sued the ever-loving snot out of this doctor, but at the time I was so relieved that she was perfect and healing and fine that I didn't pursue any legal routes. Incidentally, this doctor discontinued his practice soon afterwards, so I assume that his appetite for luncheons and golf finally caught up with him.

We have yet to hear the end of Courtney's traumatic entrance into the world. She loves to pull her birth story out and just lay on the guilt when she's in a bind or is campaigning heavily for something she wants. "Well, you know my collarbone was broken when I was born," she'll say, "and I think that you should just be glad I'm here at all, and..." This child was born with a feisty, brilliant spirit, thank God, and by the time she was three, I called her "little wise eyes."

A mass of blonde curls and wit and focus, she was on the road with me for a year and a half when I toured with Sandi Patty. The poor child also uses the fact that she was potty-trained on a bus to get more sympathy. Well, who could blame her?

We are so close now, and as I see college looming in the near future, I can barely stand it. I used to tackle her on her bed at night and say, "Stop growing up! I only have five more years left with you here at home!" And she would laugh and tell me to move and say, "Mommie Dearie, I can't stop my living!"

Courtney was the type of child—and is now the type of young woman—who sees through to the heart and core of conversations and people. She's been given the true gifts of discernment and bluntness. She's always been able to confront me with questions, and she's never let me off the hook—not even once.

During the divorce, which happened when Courtney was six years old, I had to work constantly at keeping her from trying to fix things and take care of me. She grew up too fast, knew too much too soon, always seemed older than her years. But she is a deep well, full of creativity and dreams and a love of the arts and sports. She maintains a perfect four-point average in honors classes while playing high-level volleyball and acting in plays. Gorgeous, tall, and scared to death deep down, my Courtney is quiet until she's safe...and then she opens up with a wild sense of humor and carefully-selected affection.

Through my divorce and depression I have, of course, worried about her obvious pain and recovery. When she was in the second grade, a wonderful private Christian school had a space open up three days before school started. We didn't know a soul at the school. But when I asked her if she wanted to go there, if she wanted to go for it, she looked me square in the eye and said, "Yes!" This school—the parents who took her under their wing and watched out for her with me, the friends she made there—was like God's hand upon our life.

I watched Courtney grow close to her childhood best friend, Christa, who lived across the street. I marveled at the plays and songs they wrote and acted out together. It reminded me of what I used to do as a child. Christa's family became like the arm of God around us during those years. God showed me over and over again how He was building cocoons around my daughter in the middle of her being a child of divorce.

When in the sixth grade she was asked who her role models were, she said, "Anne Frank and my mom." Frightened and thrilled, I realized she was watching my every step and that she'd seen me fall flat on my face many times. How could I be a role model? With God's good grace and a healthy dose of denial, perhaps?

Over the years, Courtney started coming into my room and helping herself to my clothes. If I have on something that she likes, she'll ask, "Are you going to wear that?" I'll reply,

"Well, I have it on. What does it look like?" And then from Courtney: "Mommie Dearie, can't I please wear it some-time...please?" Off comes the skirt or shirt or jeans, and I give in to her like the hopeless victim of a child who has made me proud in the middle of a lot of painful years—which is what I am.

The Christmas before I remarried, my daughter gave me the best gift I've ever received. She was 14 that year, and she would not open her presents until I opened her gift to me. It was a book she had put together for me. I cannot show you the pictures inside it, but let me share some of what she wrote:

Mommy, we love you so much. You mean the world to us. (Pictures of her and her brother.) We've done so many things together. (Pictures of us on vacation.) You've watched us grow and grow...I love being your daughter. When you smile, I smile...when you write, I write. You're my superhero and friend. (Picture of the two of us doing a play where we wore noses like witches. Then a piece from her language class in school written on my birthday years before.) I understand you are busy....

Musicians sacrifice many things for their work. They go to a lot of rehearsals for many hours. When they go away, they miss their families a lot! Sometimes they travel all around the world! They record music in studios...they have to be able to read music. Sometimes they spend all night at a recording studio! Everything in singing is not a piece of cake!!!!

You've done so much for me. How could I ever repay you? Mommy, you deserve to live in a castle! You're sweeter than candy! Anyway, I guess what I'm trying to say is...MOM, you are the BEST! Above all, always trust in God. God loves you! And you know I'll always be your little girl. Because I love you...family...

My fears about who Courtney might become as a child of divorce still linger. I've prayed since she was very little for the boy growing up who might one day be her husband. I pray for his journey to be lined with moments of grace and humility that will cause him to grow into a man who will love my daughter well. I want her to have a rich, healthy, real marriage. I want her to find her next place of dreaming and I want her to hold fast to the courage she has in who God has made her to be.

God continues to show me that He "loves His girls who are hurting," as my friend Nancy says. He loves me, He loves my daughter, and He has gotten us through my single-parenting years. I know I wasn't always perfect. Courtney knows it, too. Yet the rest of her life will be determined by mostly her own choices, and I pray she's learned, by watching my mistakes, where the pitfalls are. I'm grateful she knows where Jesus can be found.

Courtney turned 16 last fall, and on that day she shared another piece of writing with me—something she had written for a class assignment about someone she admired a great deal. That someone was me. I wept. She laughed. We ordered fast food.

Later, we celebrated her birthday at a dinner where the guests included her father, his wife, my new husband, her brother, and me. It was strange. It was doable. It was peaceful. We gave her the keys to her first car and a purity ring with opals and diamonds that symbolized our prayers for her together. It felt nuts. But it also felt like crazy grace.

Chariots of Fire

~

God broke the mold when He made Graham Thomas Keen.

Graham is the kind of kid who walks into a Toys "R" Us store, breathes deeply, exhales, and exclaims, "Aah! Fresh toys!" At age four, after watching a video of Mikhail Baryshnikov dancing the *Nutcracker*, he stared at the leaping, jumping, brilliant dancer and said, "Mom, that guy sure has to go potty!"

Graham sings like a bird—he was already doing session work by age ten—and loves theater. He's starred in a local production of *Oliver*, yet he also reads an atlas as if it were a sci-fi thriller. He loves *Star Wars*, but can also tell you the location of nearly any river in any obscure country of the world. This pretty much astounds his teachers and puts off the other sixth-grade boys who can't figure this kid out.

I can't figure him out, either. He's truly a rare one. He talks a mile a minute, like his Aunt Amy, and yaps away until we beg him to stop. (Amy, by the way, is smitten with Graham. They have a bond between them that started at birth. When he played the Mock Turtle in *Alice in Wonderland*, she began to call him "MT." And he loves to tease her by calling her "Old What's-Her-Name.") I wonder with amazement—and some good prayers thrown in—where my son will go and who he'll be. My new solo album is called *Marked for Life*. Graham, howling, calls it "Scarred for Life."

I wouldn't change a single thing about him.

Graham was born in 1988, miraculously with no broken bones! Or maybe not so miraculously—a different doctor than the one who delivered Courtney eased my son into this world. He was a bundle of smiles and as fat as Jabba the Hutt. By six months of age, he weighed 25 pounds and I could barely carry him around. A tumbling jumble of white-blonde curls and sparkling blue eyes, Graham laughed easily from the start— and still does. Courtney played out the role of older sister to perfection, loving and doting on her baby brother—as well as tripping him when he toddled by. I too gave my younger brother a hard time, and so the legacy continues.

When Graham was a toddler, I'd find him hiding in the pantry with the canned goods, grinning and just waiting for me to open the door. There's something about hiding and scaring me that has always brought him pleasure. Every time I came home from work, I'd hear him scurry to hide behind the furniture, anticipating my "Where could Graham be?"

He adores his big sister...always has. Courtney puts up with this better on some days than on others. Lately, she closes her door and occasionally yells out, "Dork!" But she's put up with a lot. When Graham was nine years old and playing around with how the vibrato in his voice sounded, he once decided to use a *lot* of it while singing "Amazing Grace" at the top of his lungs. Back went his head and he hit the high notes, at which point I heard Courtney's voice from upstairs: "*Make him stop!*"

And also there came the season when Courtney began to spend more time in her room, journaling and talking on the phone and being alone. She wasn't hanging out with Graham and me in the den very much anymore, and one day I started crying. "I miss Courtney," I said. "I miss Sissy, too," Graham started crying. And there we were—crying away, missing Courtney while she was only a few feet away upstairs in her room. But we knew that she was growing up, that things were changing.

I have conversations between my children captured in my mind as forever moments, like the time I overheard them actually getting along and discussing a girl who had a crush on fifth-grade Graham. Graham was asking Courtney what he should do, and Courtney calmly told her little brother, "Graham, just break up with her." (*Break up what?* I wondered.) Then she went on: "Just tell her you need your space." Graham heartily agreed, and that was that.

Graham has always been extremely confident in fighting for his viewpoint on any subject. And this gift of wisdom came to him at a young age. He even gave me some advice one day when Courtney, hormonal and upset, made a tearful exit from the car after a difficult interchange. Graham leaned forward and said in all of his nine-year-old wisdom, "Mom, don't worry about Courtney. She's 13. She's very complicated. She should come with a manual."

On a more serious note, Graham was two years old when I went through my divorce, and quite frankly, he just doesn't have any memories of his father and me together. His grief has been more open and has taken a different shape than Courtney's. When he was about seven, he began to cry and ask why his family was different. He wanted to know why we couldn't get back together. As he's gotten older, he simply grieves the unchangeable fact that he will never remember us as a whole family. It breaks my heart to see him hurting.

Ten years after the divorce, Graham asked, "Mom, did you and dad have any fun together at all?" And I realized that I could share my past—our past—with him through stories and memories. It was really healing for me to tell Graham about how Daniel would make me laugh and how we had adventures together. How we worked and traveled together and had our first home, then our second. How his dad and I loved Graham and Courtney with every piece of passion we had. Graham's face lit up with some relief as I talked, and I saw that I was giving him a piece of his history, something he craved for his own healing.

"There are times your father and I had together that nothing will ever erase," I told him. "And the divorce does not cancel that out. The good years, the moments when we were truly loving and happy, will always be times I cherish too. Nothing can rob you or me of them."

I have of course worried about Graham not having enough exposure to good, solid ongoing male companion-ship. The thought of renting a couple truck drivers or weightlifters to just drop by once a month or so even crossed my mind. Poor Graham spent ten years surrounded by dolls and lace and too much wallpaper. He still went crazy over dinosaurs and cars, but he also played readily with the puppet stage and several beheaded Barbies.

And along the way, the Lord showed me how He would father my children in ways I might not even imagine—like the time Graham went to basketball camp.

Graham attended his first school basketball camp when he was seven. He didn't know any of the other little guys in the program, but he threw himself into the adventure with everything he had. He had a kind of tenacity that year that inspired him to try new things. All week long he came home telling stories about what he was learning. Then he'd shoot baskets at our hoop at home. By the end of the week, he was very excited about the last day of camp. He knew the coaches were going to give out ribbons—and one special trophy for the best all-around player. The morning of the big day, he told me, "Mom, I prayed to the Lord this morning that I'd be all right if I didn't get the trophy—it's okay no matter what happens." I loved his attitude, even though I didn't believe a word of it. (Of course, this is a child who mirrors my emotional responses, who after my descent into clinical depression had his own child's version of one as soon as I was on the road to getting well.)

So even though I knew Graham wanted this trophy—and that his chances of getting it were slim—I secretly wanted him to win in the worst way.

The Olympics couldn't have been more thrilling than that day in June, with all of the players sitting on the floor, uncharacteristically quiet with anticipation. One by one they were given ribbons, and then one wonderful coach stood up and said, "There is one boy who showed a special attitude this week in his spirit and learning. The trophy goes to Graham Keen."

The *Chariots of Fire* music turned way up in my mind, and I fought back the tears that came to my eyes as I watched my son's face just light up. As Graham was congratulated by his friends and their parents, I somehow managed not to tackle that coach and kiss him right there in front of God and everybody.

No doubt about it. The Lord was taking care of putting those male influences in Graham's life. No need for me to hire those beefy truck drivers and weightlifters after all.

Presently, Graham visits with his father, and their love for each other grows. And he also has the great gift of my new husband, Brent, in his life. Graham now wakes up and goes to sleep with the influence of a strong and godly cowboy recording producer/engineer in his life. Brent is opening up a whole new world of horses and fishing and paddleboats and life on a farm to Graham while still appreciating my son's amazing talents. Brent is also tougher on Graham than I am, and this is another blessing in the life of the "motor mouth of the South" (again, like his Aunt Amy), who will argue about anything at the drop of a hat.

I see God's covering over my Graham's heart and life. I see the gifting and the wild assortment of interests that have been planted in him.

Eight years of single parenting taught me this one price-less lesson: My children were God's before they were mine. They are still His. And His love fills in the spaces and places left blank, spaces that not one nor even two parents can fill in. Because some days parenting just has to be trusted to God's watchful eye. And He never tires, never sleeps, and never gives up on these wonders called children, wonders that He allows us to have and to hold for a season.

Traditions Redeemed

~

Here I am again, snookered by a 16-year-old green-eyed persuasion named Courtney to make the yearly trek to Florida for spring break. Her plan for this year, the most courageous plan to date, includes bringing along three other gorgeous 16-year-old friends and her younger brother Graham, who I insist is part of the package. Brent, my husband of two years, is engineering a recording with Ricky Skaggs this week on a Bill Monroe tribute project. I imagine he's silently grateful to have a legitimate excuse for missing the long drive to the beach in a van full of hormonal young women and one very special but very talkative man-child.

I've been down this road before. Oh, yeah. For years I've spent hundreds of dollars on this kind of thing—the condo on the beach, a time brought on by good grades and endless comments along the lines of "Mom, we need to have fun!" For years I've been dismally disappointed by paying top dollar to watch it rain for a week in Florida. We've shivered and, with teeth chattering, declared our "good time" along with all the rest of the families in denial. Suffice it to say, I've had it with the spring break dream. In fact, this year I told Courtney that I think I have a full-fledged phobia surrounding the whole idea of anything good coming from being down south in March.

The last trip was the phobia-inducer. With a shred of naivete still left, I was hopeful enough to follow the crowd from my kids' school to the beach, driving down the freeway like a modern-day captive in search of the promised land.

Retrospectively, it was more like being a sheep led to the shearing—the shredding of my pocketbook, with my credit cards blazing. Little did I know that my expensive condo would be *the* hangout for an army of kids, quarantined inside by the rain. And that some unknown force would instruct these kids to eat everything I had in the fridge. Dutifully, they stepped all over the furniture, watched the TV with the volume on "stun," and left a pile of dirty, sandy tennis shoes at my front door each day. All I wanted out of the deal was a little peace and quiet and a respectable sunburn.

But it got worse. In addition to the teenagers on parade, I also acquired the uninvited company of an old friend who was going through a divorce. Like the teenagers, he decided that my place was the place to be, and—resembling the teenagers once again—he kept begging me to reassure him of his attractiveness. On top of this, he didn't know that I knew he was seeing another woman in another state, and that he was dragging his soon-to-be ex-wife—and my dear friend—through all sorts of torment.

The week became a blur—a series of days filled with endless noise, sinus problems brought on by the cold weather, and way too many people—until one day I found myself driving the van aimlessly through the rain in an attempt to avoid being a character in my own beach getaway.

Admittedly, there *was* the one day the sun almost appeared. I rented a chair/umbrella setup and took out my pile of favorite books, ready to soak in the good time. No sooner had I sat down, determined to smile and make the best of things, than the sun began a devilish dance in and out of the clouds. The weather that day was borderline at best. When the sun was shining, my goosebumps would settle down from resembling Mount Everest to looking like a few hills in Scotland. I had a sweatshirt handy and a large towel, both of which I was forced to wrap myself in over and over again. Between the freeze zones, when the sun peeked out, I threw everything off in a desperate attempt to get some vitamin D somewhere on my oh-so-white body. Several hours later I realized that I was the only one still on the beach sitting under a useless umbrella and pretending that it was a nice day. The guy working the umbrella stand looked as if he wished I would go in so he could go home. His lips were blue. One can deny retreat for only so long.

This year, however, a miracle occurred. The sun actually is out. It's above 65 degrees, and after a few days of being here, I understand why we mortals take this risk year after year in hopes of a few days like the ones we've had this time. God smiled on our spring break—or maybe one of those girls I brought is an angel in disguise. Maybe it was just a matter of rolling the dice long enough so we could finally hit the beach without being in danger of suffering frostbite. Whatever the reason, I am grateful for the tan lines and pink noses all around me. I am grateful to watch Graham build sand castles as seagulls swoop down to inspect his creation. I am grateful to see Courtney playing volleyball with her friends. Of course, I do understand the rules about Mommie Dearie staying a respectable distance away, but I'm always close enough to witness the teenage drama that plays out a few yards away.

And for a few moments this week, just sitting and being and staring at the ocean, I understood again the comfort of this experience, of just being in the presence of this vast and powerful blue-green water. It could sweep us all away if the tide so turned—and it could lap at us like a dog playing with children, or sing like a lullaby the repeated sound of waves meeting shore. It all boils down to the primal child/earth creatures that we are. Something in us longs for something larger, something unexplainable. For my children, who spend countless hours writing essays, pondering math problems, and putting together science projects, it is therapeutic to be confronted with an ocean that cannot be explained—only experienced and enjoyed. How faithful God is to honor one Olympic step in the right direction and make it worth everything.

Florida excluded, there are so many traditions God redeemed for me over the years as I blindly stumbled through the process of trying to create a safe new home for my children and me. The yearly trek to Florida began soon after my divorce, and it has continued. But along with Florida, we've created other traditions as well. Smaller than spring break, but certainly just as meaningful.

After the divorce, my children began to do the same thing my brother and I had done as kids—sleep under the Christmas tree on December twenty-third, the eve of Christmas Eve. Don't ask me why, but I adored doing this as a child—staring up at the lights all night, waking up and knowing that in a couple of days presents would magically appear in my special sleeping spot.

As it turned out, Courtney and Graham also loved doing this. And we added our own twist to this tradition. We made Christmas sugar cookies before the tree-sleeping event, decorating them with this colorful, squeeze-tube kind of icing (store-bought—I refuse to make that from scratch!). Courtney and Graham each had a stash of homemade cookies to eat under the tree, and they would leave some for Santa on the hearth along with milk. The funny part is that these cookies were so revered, such works of art, that everyone was afraid to eat any. They were usually stale by January and were thrown away little by little. However, Santa usually managed to put away his cookies with no problem at all.

My children also have a sweet tradition of taking care of me, little moments here and there. One of these favorite moments happened when I arrived home after a long day in the studio. There stood Courtney, wearing my elegant black dress from high school complete with my white linen apron. She had coerced Graham into putting on a suit and setting the table in the dining room. Together they'd cleared the fridge of its leftovers—stuff like cauliflower and yogurt—to create a restaurant experience for me to come home to. They named the restaurant Lendel's Fine Dining (the fine part being debatable).

Ushered into Lendel's and given a handwritten menu, I was served like a queen. I was so moved by their creativity and love and how God was giving us "forever" moments in the middle of hard times that I actually choked down the strange combination of foods. Graham had set up a cash register, where I paid with pretend money, and I took pictures of them in uniform, standing outside in the August sunshine. I still bring these treasured pictures with me when I am on the road.

My favorite tradition, one of the signs that showed me God was healing us, was Courtney's good-night to Graham and me: "Good-night, *family*." The way she called herself, Graham, and me "family" brought me such great comfort. It was the pronouncement of her making peace with being just the three of us—the new configuration and the new hope God had given us in our present and for our future.

The yearly trips to Florida have had to be the hardest new tradition for me to take on. It took a long time before I was brave enough to take the kids on vacation by myself. When I finally did venture out and take them on weekend trips—and then ultimately to Florida—it was amazing to see how God took such tender care of us.

I made my last trip to Florida as a single mom after a pitiful attempt at a yard sale. I hate yard sales, but I was at my wit's end. After all the effort, I'd made $150 and had seen more people than I'd wanted to—people who didn't want my little offering of used clothes and household items. By the end of the day, I was fighting back tears and giving away boxes of "treasures." I realized that's what I should have done all along—slept in and made a leisurely trip to the Goodwill.

Our garage sale profits in my wallet, the kids and I packed up for a three-day trip to the beach. Single, almost flat-broke, and with a kidney infection on top of it all, I nonetheless put the pedal to the metal. My kids were going to see the ocean that year if it killed me.

When we arrived, it was late, the rental office was closed, and I couldn't find the key to the condo. It was raining. Courtney and Graham were not exactly getting along. Chaos ruled. I stalled and took us to dinner at a nearby restaurant and tried to think of how I might find the key to the condo and what I might say, without losing my religion, to the rental agent about leaving us stranded.

When I went outside to use the phone booth again, I dropped the case that held my credit cards and money in the mud. That did it. I lost it. Crying and picking up the muddy cards, I started in on God: "What do You expect from me? What am I doing wrong? Why can't I get a little help here? Just a break now and then?"

As is often the case with me, I make things worse when I panic. The key had been left for us pending a late arrival. We retrieved it and scampered into our condo, relieved and hoping for a good time.

The next few days were good—good but bittersweet. Everywhere I looked, I saw families together swimming and playing and having fun. It looked like I was the only single mom around. Thankfully, I was awake enough to enjoy the miracle of watching my two children play in the waves with joy and complete abandon. But when they were not close by, I walked out into the waves and stared into the heavens and cried out to God, "If all things work together for good, I've missed the good part! I'm so broke, I have no business being here. And I have no idea where You'd have me go from here...Romans 8, Romans 8...all things work together for good for those that love You...I do love You. Where are You? I can't find You anymore!"

What I didn't know was that God was working hard, taking care of me and preparing me for Brent. At that time my second husband's world was coming apart at the seams.

There was much eternal work being done as I stood in the ocean.

This spring break, many years later, I cannot help but remember that summer. Each time I see this coastline at this particular beautiful place on the gulf, I think of my cries to God. The clouds were so lovely and the water sparkled, but my soul was so lifeless and weak. Yet, as the writer Anne Lamott says, "I do not at all understand the mystery of grace—only that it meets us where we are but does not leave us where it found us."

My beach-excursion phobia is lessening over time. And the mystery of grace is growing. I'm just now beginning to understand that God's ways truly are not our own, but they are to be trusted and not to be doubted. He cares about all kinds of things—even the silly things like sleeping under Christmas trees and eating leftovers made elegant and sitting stubbornly under umbrellas on cloudy beaches. Nothing falls through His hands without His tears or smiles mixed in. Who knew that even spring breaks can be redeemed, that traditions can be revised and grow?

One night, years before my life seemed to begin again, I sat in the house at dusk, listening to both of my children singing in their rooms. Courtney was singing along with a *Les Miserables* soundtrack, while Graham was happily barreling through the national anthem. For a moment I was astonished. Somehow, in the middle of having no money, putting up with a revolving-door traveling mom, and living in a broken home, my children were singing.

Funny. We didn't seem broken.

Or maybe this type of brokenness can be holy.

Rock Flowers

~

New turf. New soil in my life and heart. In November of 1999, the arrival of two little girls gave me another chance to learn how to be more fully human and full of grace. Twins were born to my ex-husband and his wife. They arrived seven weeks early, and their prematurity compounded the rest of the emotional upheaval that the miracle of birth unleashes on a family.

Courtney received a call on her phone in her room from her father, who announced the birth of the babies. It had happened for him as he was rushing back into town. His wife, caught in labor unawares, went to the hospital alone. Thankfully, God granted her the gift of a friend who was a nurse on duty at the time, so she was not left completely to her own private prayers and fears during the emergency C-section that left both her and the twins at great risk of complications—even death. My children's stepmother actually "crashed" on the operating table and was in intensive care for several days.

I thought I was prepared for the news of the twins' birth. My children and I had talked about the feelings we had about their new siblings—half-siblings—the new family my ex-husband was about to receive. We thought that almost nine months of preparation would groom us for the shock, acceptance, and genuine joy of the upcoming event. My ex-husband and his wife had gone through many excruciating years of infertility treatment, and the news of the pregnancy—twins, no less—was overwhelming with implications of every kind. There would be the adjustment of my children to the intrusion and inclusion of two new sisters. There would be the adjustment for my ex-husband to an entirely new second family.

And there would be my adjustment as well. We all prayed together and seemed as prepared as any new family can be.

Complicating things was the awareness that my new husband, Brent, had lost a child in his divorce. His beloved son of almost five years was declared the child of another man who his wife had been secretly seeing. In the wake of the DNA tests and the nightmare of his divorce, he watched his ex-wife and son drive away with the "real" father. And so I knew that Brent had hoped and prayed that he and I might be one of those miracle Abraham-and-Sarah couples, having babies well into our later years. Now he was dealing with my ex-husband becoming a father yet again. How would my precious husband handle his own feelings about this transition, this unknown soul-space where comedy and tragedy intersect?

When the news of the twins' birth came that night, I was bowled over by my own flood of emotions. I spoke with my ex-husband privately after he'd talked to our children, and I heard the fear in his voice when he talked about the health of his wife and new daughters. It was touch and go. There was no guarantee that this would be a happy little journey from hospital to home. And more than anything, I realized that a miracle of birth had happened for me as well as for him.

Of course, there was the initial shock and inability to compute the reality that my children had siblings...half-sisters! Courtney smiled at me calmly from the second floor, announced she had two sisters, and then walked back to her room. Sisters! Graham threw himself on the floor and wailed, "Two more sisters! I can't take two more sisters!"

My children had other siblings—siblings not born of my body. Yet a part of their father would forever be a part of me and a part of them.

I was blindsided by the upheaval in my heart. But most surprising and pleasing of all was the dawning of true healing in my soul. How could it be that, more than anything in the world, I wanted everything to be all right? After the weird, out-of-body strangeness of talking to the father of my children about *his* new children, I was incredulous as I realized that I was filled with an intense prayer for God to have mercy on this new family. Admittedly there were a few waves of jealousy, but they were quickly replaced with a sincere desire that all be well.

For days I prayed for the condition of my children's stepmother as she moved from the intensive care to the stable unit and then finally home. She is a good stepmother to my children, and over and over in a mixture of unexplainable feelings, the overriding tide turned toward mercy.

Now, this did not happen because I am any kind of good person. Quite the contrary. I am as capable of bitterness as anyone else. I did not grow stoic armor around my heart or turn into some martyr for the greater good of my children. This miracle in my psyche was an act of God. There is no other explanation. And its gestation must have been much longer than nine months. It was more like nine years—nine years of giving up and letting go. Falling down and asking for guidance. Doing things the wrong way, then trying again and doing them halfway right, then falling down again.

Forgiveness—and grace—make it real somehow.

When the twins came home, when everyone was out of the woods and the babies were allowed to have visitors, I was one of the first at the door. My ex-husband asked me to come. I looked at the girls with wonder and gratitude, seeing that they were perfect and well. Their mother was recovering and getting stronger. Yes, I was somewhat uncomfortable...but to my core, so very grateful.

Only God's grace can allow seeds of unconditional love to grow in the shallow ground of defeat. I think of the flowers that grow in rocky places where there is no soil. These flowers grow despite never being fertilized or nurtured. These flowers thrive and live as a testament of God's good grace to His earth. And maybe the rock flowers grow to remind us that, indeed, there is a place of healing in each of us where rock flowers can bloom.

One
COLORS

Two
RED

Three
ORANGE

Four
YELLOW

Five
GREEN

Six
BLUE

Seven
PURPLE

Eight
RAINBOW

You must ask for God's help. Even when you have done so, it may seem to you for a long time that no help…is being given. Never mind. After each failure, ask forgiveness, pick yourself up, and try again.… This process trains us in the habits of the soul which are more important [than any virtue]. It cures our illusions about ourselves and teaches us to depend on God.

—C.S. Lewis, *Mere Christianity*

1994

Reading about the life of C.S. Lewis, I find tremendous joy in his Joy! God gave one of the greatest theologians of our time a divorced woman to love!

1994

Prayer: "God, may I draw even closer to You. May You be the shoulder I lean on, the reason I get up every day, the one I cry to and shake my fist at and have an active, passionate, real relationship with. But, dear Father, may I someday have a companion here—a man to hold me and a safe place to share my heart."

Summer, 1994

Once again, feeling some semblance of peace. Like God is my shepherd, and I'm not afraid of my age and being alone. I just want to do what is right for my children.

Late summer, 1994

What are God's ways? Who can know? Suddenly He moves, comes, builds character in us in seasons of blinding pain. He teaches, gives, breathes in us, and then there is a place to rest until the next season of pain. Life is full of turmoil and hardship. I can walk with God through it or walk alone. I choose to embrace where I am, knowing God is sovereign. I can't learn or see it; I just have to believe that He is working somehow.

December, 1994

Please let me have someone in my life again, Lord—a husband, someone like You created me to desire. I want a family...please don't ask me to be single forever, to live alone...please, please don't break me that much!

December, 1994

Could it be that whatever it is God is working in me has to be accomplished by my heart being broken and full of pain? If so, then I'm scared of God and His love. If I try to do His will, does that mean I will be broken more and more? I'm scared I'll lose heart.

December, 1994

Important lessons to be learned from my dating experiences thus far:

1. Don't let intimacy go before commitment.
2. Don't compromise on what kind of man you are waiting for.
3. Try not to doubt God's faithfulness because of failed relationships.
4. Do not punish yourself for opening your heart again.

December, 1994

Maybe my desire for a husband has become something of an idol that needs tearing down....

Summer, 1995

I broke off the engagement to J.P. The writer Joyce Meyer says that God gives us grace enough for each situation in our lives—just enough to do what is required, and then the grace is lifted. It was hard to hurt someone again by jumping ahead of God, but I know this marriage would be wrong. I would have tried hard to please him, and I know he loves me, but I'm not in love.

End of year, 1995

I had hoped and prayed that I might have an answer in my desire for a companion by now, without another Christmas alone. Yet I believe the answer must be that it's not time. God has other things for me now.

1996

I will continue to plead before my Lord for Him to remember me a husband, and until then I will try to hold myself together by relying on His strength. A dream clutched too tightly becomes an idol.

"Isaac"

I have a prayer as pure as gold
That where You lead me I will go
And I'll not miss the impassioned plea
When Your sweet Spirit calls to me

And in that hour and in that time
When I must lose my will in Thine
O my allegiance will be found
The day I lay my Isaac down

Grant me a faith beyond all doubt
Whose flames of hope cannot burn out
Let mercy flow and grace abound
The day I lay my Isaac down

Sweet Lamb of love most blessed friend
Nailed to the altar for my sin
Where in my place God's son was bound
The day He laid His Jesus down

Each idol vain is now laid bare
His suffering cross my heart will share
Earth's kingdoms fall without a sound
The day I lay my Isaac down
My soul redeemed on holy ground
The day I lay my Isaac down.

—Bonnie Keen

Bringing Up Eve

~

Blessed (happy, to be envied) is she who believed
that there would be a fulfillment of the things that
were spoken to her from the Lord. And Mary said,
My soul magnifies and extols the Lord.

—LUKE 1:45,46 AMP

Sometimes I look around me and am struck by how many husbandless women I know—and some of these women are still married! So many of us seem to be longing for the same things Eve longed for in the garden all those years ago—companionship, love, peace, control over our circumstances. Modern-day widowhood—loneliness—is on the rise. A race of women is trying to find its way in a world of men.

Stripped down to the bare bones, the issues remain the same. Choices are still choices. Free will is still free will. And as women, we still seem to have the same needs that began with Eve. We long for a man to love and hold us—in a world we can both submit to and have control of.

Our culture would have us believe that Eve can have it all—hearth, home, family, and job—if she plays it right. Of course, she always has the alternative of having children without home or marriage, or just making a career with a significant other (either sex—your choice), complete with stock options and no commitments. Better yet, she could live the life of highest evolution—needing no one and nothing but herself. She can "find the god within herself" and "be for herself all she really needs."

Unfortunately for all the Eves out there, the original lie—the "I can be God" lie—is still alive and well. Couched in beautiful, intellectual rhetoric, this lie is embraced by some of the most famous Eves of our day. And although I don't wish to lay all the blame at their feet, I do believe that many of today's role models are the saddest people around. Our culture likes to take those who have talent in the arts, elevate them to godlike status, and assume that they must have the answers to the mysteries—the answers that elude the rest of us common folk.

When did beauty, success, and just plain willful ego ever guarantee a depth of soul or spirit?

My teenage daughter is now in the process of defining who she is. I watch as Courtney weighs the input she receives from every source about what it means to be fully woman. It seems that, more than ever, the women in her generation will need to look to God to give their lives true definition and purpose. She's reading Joshua Harris's book *I Kissed Dating Goodbye*. It's a book that offers a radical, provocative, Christian perspective on our American dating scene. It was her own decision to read the book, and I am thankful that she is searching for God's voice in the middle of all the other voices that scream out for her attention.

It is complicated to be on the brink of womanhood. It is complicated to be a woman. When I see what comes calling at the door through television, advertising, and the like, it truly frightens me. The Eves of our day seem as deluded as the original Eve, and I long for my Courtney—and other women, too—to find themselves through the movement of the Maker's Spirit, not through voices that define love, romance, motherhood, and vocation without the filter of God's truth.

I once heard it said that our self-esteem will be largely determined by what the most important person in our life thinks of us. Whoever this person might be—God, spouse, friend, parent, or business partner—how he or she sees us has a tremendous impact on how we see ourselves. And our self-esteem dictates the quality of human beings we align ourselves with in marriage and in friendship.

We're bombarded from every side with an airbrushed, high-gloss prototype of the "successful" woman. She's hip and altogether free. And I think an image of her is revered, in a subtle light, in certain Christian settings—an image that claims we should have a certain degree of opulence to be a real Christian woman.

Where has the original dream gone?

I believe we were created to find our greatest fulfillment in being uniquely ourselves, in being cherished as a vital part of a man's life—a man we are wholly committed to before God. More than anything, women have the right to delight in the differences among each other. We were made to be celebrated for the very qualities that our culture has tried to deny us. Woman, at her core, is lovely and soft, yet strong in her ability, able to bear up under everything from the common cold to juggling a thousand things at once. She is able to carry out the childbearing, life-nurturing part of God's plan, not from under the foot of Adam, but by his side—cherished and protected.

It saddens me to hear some of my stay-at-home-mom friends apologize for not working outside the home and instead staying home to care for their young children. A woman's role today is jumbled and tumbled. Men are confused about what women want, and who can blame them? Pride has kept us from being able to openly value each other for our differences. I wonder if by focusing on "equality" as a woman's goal, we have thus handicapped ourselves to a point where there are more divorces and more lonely, single women than ever.

My Courtney has "wise eyes." She was born with them. Even as a little girl, she could size up almost any person and any situation with an uncanny frankness. It's a trait I wish I had. One day, after years of watching me run around like a maniac, trying to be both father and mother and winding up exhausted most of the time, Courtney looked at me with great tenderness but also with direct assurance and said, "I'm not going to do what you've done. I don't want to do everything. I want a different life."

Thank God for my daughter's clarity! And I applaud her perspective. Single momhood has proven to me that none of us were made to walk this path of parenthood alone. But I do have some help—a manual that helps me to discover the full capacity of womanhood. Instead of studying the garbage that flies at me from mainstream magazine racks, I prefer to study what the Word of God says.

It's so very difficult to separate our pain from the desire to be loved. As I listen to my sisters in Christ and watch marriages fall apart all around me, I believe that Eve has become a modern-day widow. She knows the pain of loneliness and the fear of single parenthood. She walks through the aftermath of divorce—betrayal, loss, disappointment, financial devastation.

At every concert of mine and in private conversations with so many people, I hear the resounding cry of pain, loneliness, and questions. This condition of spouseless, loveless living is shared by so many.

Through my own widow years, the Lord allowed me to learn how to accept love and how to be at peace with even the "nos" of my God. I learned how to love a God who is big enough to disappoint me. Yielding to and living in the reality of the "no," yet still praying with a hopeful heart for the "yes," was a hard pill for me to swallow. But strangely it brought me comfort.

At the end of the day, every Eve—the widow, the single parent, the woman who feels lonely or rejected—is desperately in need of her God. Where the need is great, His grace flows in abundance. For He embodies the passion of all that is truly male and compelling. The Lord continues to woo us back to Himself and to reveal Himself as our first husband: "Don't be afraid, because you will not be ashamed. Don't be embarrassed, because you will not be disgraced. You will forget the shame you felt earlier; you will not remember the shame you felt when you lost your husband. The God who made you is like your husband. His name is the LORD All-Powerful. The Holy One of Israel is the one who saves you. He is called the God of all the earth. You were like a woman whose husband left her, and you were very sad. You were like a wife who married young and then her husband left her. But the LORD called you to be his... I left you for a short time, but with great kindness I will bring you back again."

There was a time when the whole notion of God's being my husband made me absolutely furious. God is God and Spirit, and I longed for a human husband's comfort and touch. But it wasn't until I had walked through enough pain of my own choosing, enough counterfeit relationships, that I discovered my first and real husband can only be found in God—when I'm in His arms. I discovered that even stronger than my passion for human love is my desperate thirst to be intimate with my Maker.

My vision of love expanded and grew and was laid on the altar and given over to the lordship of Christ many times. God was faithful to refine my vision through the fires of His grace and purposes. It's been vitally important for me to have this vision—this hope in the middle of hopelessness. This hope demands that I align my heart's desires with God's dreams for me—especially when I am ever-so-aware of my own failures and my own need for mercy. The same unchanging love and mercy that gave us breath and life, that endowed our bodies with the beautiful ability to bear children, that poured down a special gift of nurturing and affection into our hands and hearts, is still—evermore and everlasting—the same.

Widowhood is not the end of the story.

God allowed me to trust Him with my pain, my anger, and my frustrations. He was a coparent with me, in silent and not-so-silent partnership—as the husband I needed and the father my children needed. With a loving, strong presence, He comforted me in the most unlikely moments—especially when I was about to give up.

It is my prayer that we as women will never lose sight of the hope we have as we walk covered by the blood of Christ. Our legacy is the mark we wear, what we were given in the beginning—the mark and the brand of life and the promise of an eternity with our first love. And this first and greatest love comes from our Father God, who while holding us close and claiming us as His own, allows us room and grace to continue to dream.

Insanity

~

Did Jesus die so all of us could just hang on by our fingernails?

At times I look at my own life and the lives of my close friends and see so little evidence of our being marked for life. We seem to be, for the most part, just scraping by, just barely hanging on through the days and nights of disappointment and unanswered questions. But I wonder if maybe we have forgotten how to demand a blessing of the Lord, to engage in an honest struggle with Him.

How many of us get down in the dark, quiet minutes of the night—the time when everything is laid bare, demanding that we reckon with it—and duke it out, so to speak, with God? Is that not what David did? And Jacob? Is that not what Jesus meant when He told us to continue seeking until we find, knocking until a door opens?

It's a crazy, wild hope. But God's revelations often are given only after a time of coming face-to-face with the One we dare not see face-to-face.

As crazy as it sounds, I've begun to pray for "insanity." I want to be insanely determined to find God. The dirt will fly, the voices will rise and fall, but maybe, after I dig in my heels as deeply as I can and am at the end of myself once again, I'll be able to demand my right as a child of God—my right to be blessed.

Blessing, for me, is peace. It's contentment with wherever God has me and the ability to praise and rejoice in whatever comes while still praying and hoping for the dreams He has put in my heart. The challenge is holding on to the dreams while living with the questions.

If Einstein's theory is true that at the speed of light, time as we know it stands still, and if—based on that theory— God is outside of our timeframe, and if, as the Word says, HE IS forever I AM, and if Jesus is crucified and resurrected throughout eternity—if He *is* and *remains*—then didn't He die in order for something to *change* in me?

So I began to make a list. I called it "Things I Don't Believe Jesus Died For." I wrote down things like: "He didn't die so that I would give up on my dreams." And: "He didn't die so that the heartaches and disappointments of my life would make me bitter or defeated." And this: "He didn't die so that my children would face a hopeless journey."

Then I made another list. I called it "Things He Did Die For." And I listed all of those things—dreams that stay alive, love that I can taste, redemption.

My precious friend Karen once called me, holding on by her fingernails in a moment of trying to win God's approval, or perhaps trying to talk Him into relieving her of her present pain. I did my best to help her, as so many have helped me. We talked about the Word made flesh. God as man. His heart seen in the flesh of Jesus, who willingly died a bloody and passionate death for us. God came to win His family back—at the price of His own heart.

I cannot believe that Calvary was willingly suffered by the Son of God simply to leave us to dangle over the abyss.

And so I believe this: We are intended for communion with the God of creation. When I use the word "communion," I mean real relationship, consisting of passionate, ongoing daily conversation, arguing, asking, loving, embracing, and knowing that the One we are in this kind of relationship with is the One who will never throw up His hands and walk away.

We are to stand only on the merit of Christ's life and accomplishments. To even attempt to stand on my own life would be laughable, utter folly. But I will stand any day in the face of the enemy and defy his attempts to touch so much as a thumbnail of the ones who are covered by the blood of the Lamb. We are marked for another joy. We are marked for life.

Jesus died to give me a wild hope—some would call it insanity, perhaps—a hope that ushers in the miracle of resurrection in our lives, every day.

Understanding

~

When I think about the state of depression, several things pop into my head.

Always there's the initial thought that depression is a cop-out, an excuse, an imagined state of emotional being that allows one an assortment of reasons to release responsibility for one's actions. If one is depressed, one might have the license to overeat, oversleep, undereat, undersleep, be manic, crazed, reclusive, moody, or morbid, unable to work, unable to be required to do (or not do) anything in particular, depending on what the requirements are.

Of course this theory dissolves in mere seconds as I evaluate my own experience with depression. Facing the truth that depression is a disease silences the ignorant, rather innocent preconceptions I once had.

Disease.

The sound of that word makes me cringe a bit, and I feel the urge to argue that the whole theory is unfair. Yet I know that it is a disease, just as surely as diabetes or lupus or anything where the body is out of kilter with itself internally is a disease. Emotionally, depression is like a flu that hangs on, not going away—pulling its victim into a large, overwhelming hole of darkness. I would have called this whole thing crazy had I not dropped into this abyss myself. And the sobering aspect of the depressive condition is that, for me and countless other people of faith, it is now a part of my life that I cannot ignore or treat casually.

If I try to pull myself up by my own bootstraps of faith and hang on to strength from within myself, I can do this for a while. For a few weeks or months, I can be strong enough to sidestep the dark, gaping hole that always lurks a few feet away. Maybe if I have enough quiet time and do enough to keep myself preoccupied with other things, I can avoid the nosedive. Ultimately, however, the hole sucks me under. Any unforeseen disruption can pull me in. Any kind of grief or even happy episode can overwhelm my emotional system, triggering the basket case potential—"BCP"—that I've grown to accept, which knocks me for a loop.

> These are the poor in spirit whom Jesus declares blessed. They know how to accept a gift. "Come on, all you who are wiped out, confused, bewildered, lost, beat up, scarred, scared, threatened, depressed, and I'll enlighten your mind with wisdom and fill your heart with tenderness that I have received from my Father."
> Our hope, our acceptance of the invitation to the banquet, is not based on the idea that we are going to be free of pain and suffering. Rather, it is based on the firm conviction that we will triumph over suffering.
> —BRENNAN MANNING, *Reflections for Ragamuffins*

I use the above quotations as arguments against those who shame people like me, people who suffer off and on from varying degrees of recurring depression. Depression is like diabetes or arthritis or something that can be contained and addressed spiritually and medically, but in many cases never completely goes away.

Yes, it would be amazing to be able to believe that depression could be cured with a miracle, a laying on of hands or prayer or a casting out of demonic presence—and I do believe that all efforts should certainly be made to free the person who suffers from depression. But just as some cancer victims are prayed over and anointed with oil and lifted up and fasted over and still go to be with God, some people with depression—people who love God with their heart and soul and breath—still live for years in bouts of darkness.

We learn to praise God in the darkness. That is the hope that Brennan Manning speaks of. We know we will have triumph over suffering. It will manifest itself in God's time and in ways in which we must simply trust. This side of heaven or not.

To label a cure for depression as a simple act of repentance and spiritual deliverance is to leave the depressed person further defeated. Especially if—after giving his or her pain over to this theory and following every step laid out for healing as the church and the Word of God define it—one is left with the disease still falling like a smothering blanket over one's heart.

I would venture to say that God affirmed the existence of depression by allowing us to hear great men, men after His own heart, cry out in pain and depression in the Psalms, in the book of Job, in the words of Paul in prison, and—finally, most powerfully—in the words of God in the flesh, enduring the human condition, crying out from the cross: "My God, why hast Thou forsaken me?"

God came as man. He understands it all. Jesus pleads on our behalf at the right hand of His Father. The rest is up to us—to take our medication, to pray and lift up our condition daily, to enlighten those around us that the moods that threaten to pull us under at times are not anybody's fault, but a chemical condition that must be treated as such.

It is so important that depression be acknowledged and not explained away. In the array of depressive diseases, from clinical to situational to bipolar to schizophrenic, there are hundreds of variances. Some people suffer greatly in the winter, when they are deprived of sunlight. Something as simple as not enough sunlight can send some people into periods of great despair, unable to do basic chores, and longing only for the chance to stay in bed for days. Certain hard times endured over long periods can result in the body shutting down, with a much-diminished appetite and an inability to get enough sleep—a cycle that turns the emotional/physical state of a person into a chemical clinical depression. Many of these conditions can be effectively treated with medication, which after a time can be eliminated. However, the predisposition to depression remains and must be watched for and addressed if the signs appear again.

I guess that, more than anything, I hope that as people of faith we will not avert our eyes from those among us who wrestle with the disease of depression. These people need our help, and more than anything, they need for someone to understand they are working very hard to deal with their condition and they love the Lord as much as anyone. Probably the hardest aspect of this kind of life for depressed Christians to reconcile with their faith is why they are not able to experience joy because of their emotional state. "Why can't I just get over it?" they wonder. "If I loved God enough, I wouldn't feel this way, would I?" But I raise the possibility that any believer who goes through a difficult season—be it physical, emotional, or spiritual—asks the same thing. Yet the Lord sees beyond this. He knows, because of His sojourn on earth in the body and presence of His Son, what we go through, and I sincerely believe that He understands about our breaking points.

We were created for a perfect world. And then into this world came violence, sin, hunger, rape, murder, gossip, drunkenness, betrayal, and senseless loss. We were created to walk in the garden with our God each day, to laugh and enjoy each other as Creator and creation. But instead we find ourselves fighting for those garden moments in the middle of a less-than-perfect world.

Some people do have the ability to simply shut out the negatives of this world, as a dear friend of mine does when she holds up her hands in a time-out signal and says, "Too much sharing! Too much sharing!" Others have an innate sense of how to hear the daily news and deal with the personal challenges that come with life and "just roll with it, baby." Then there are those of us like me, who take the world into ourselves in a way that is not healthy—a way that assimilates the pain.

I was in my early twenties, making dinner one night, when I first realized that I needed to monitor how much of the evening news I could watch. There was a story about a three-year-old boy who had been sexually abused and actually killed in the process, and I literally fell to the floor weeping, unable to get up. The image of this child haunted me. I couldn't get him out of my mind.

Years later, having gone through several levels of clinical depression, I've learned the hard way to guard myself from what I see and hear as much as possible, so as not to give myself too much to process. I don't think I was made for taking in too much at a time. And I have a theory that many people who suffer from depression cannot assimilate the world as it is. With too much overload, something snaps. And on top of this, we live at a time in history when information comes to us in rapid succession from every side. Scenes of abuse and neglect and deceit greet us every time we turn on the television, go online, or pick up a newspaper. It's simply everywhere.

Depression has always been part of the condition of a fallen world. But I believe it's an epidemic now because human beings were not created by our loving God to know or deal with such grief. When God commanded Adam and

Eve not to eat from the tree of the knowledge of good and evil, I believe it was because He wanted to shield them from knowing things that they were not equipped to bear. The enemy said, "If you eat, you will be like God." Yet we cannot be like God. God knows and sees and understands that He is able to redeem and to have victory over the unworldly enormity of pain. And when Adam and Eve took that bite, the door was opened for us to see what only God—God alone—can bear.

I am of the group that must constantly spit out the fruit of that tree and keep my eyes on the One who does reign over this world. And *many* precious saints suffer deeply in this fallen condition. They are saved. They love Christ. They just were not made to hold up as well as others against the daily onslaught of the dark side in this most beautiful earth.

On the flip side of the coin, there are some people who walk through amazing loss and agony and seem almost stoic in their ability to stay balanced. I love the following words of Robert Frost: "What God does not protect us from, He uses to perfect us." It reminds me so much of my second husband, Brent, who lost two of the most precious people in his life in ways that would have sent me plummeting down.

Brent's closest and best friend was his father. When he speaks of his dad, Brent's face lights up as he goes on about how funny he was, and also how driven and successful and loving and attentive. One night when Brent was 14, his father asked him to do a chore for him. Because it was a Wednesday night, Brent told his dad that he wanted to go to church and would do the chore later. That was the last time the two of them spoke together. His father died of a sudden heart attack the next day. When I asked him how he had dealt with such a loss, Brent told me of the great friends he had had at church who had helped and supported him. But he had decided then and there that nothing would ever hurt him that badly again.

However, Brent *was* hurt again. He had been married for 17 years and was parenting a little four-year-old boy when he discovered the bitter truth that his son was another man's biological child. Once again, the person he loved most in the world was taken out of his life suddenly, this time under horrible conditions. When we talk and pray about his son, I watch as silent tears slip down Brent's face. It's a pain I know I cannot understand. Yet somehow he was able to move on without buckling, even after this horrible loss of his son and his marriage, in a way that astounds me.

"You said you learned to put up walls after your dad died so that no one would ever touch you that deeply again," I said to him recently on his son's birthday weekend. He nodded. "And yet," I went on, "here you've let me into your life and heart, and not only that, but you've reached out to embrace my children as your own!"

It seems Brent is one of those people whom this world tries to defeat. Yet the tragedies in his life have only made his heart more tender.

Early on in our marriage, my issues with depression forced Brent to deal with how he and I respond differently to stress and loss. His patience is a blessing for me, and his sense of humor is our greatest ally. He jokes and makes me laugh at what a basket case I am, and he helps me lighten up. I'm lucky to have such a mate, one who respects the struggles I have.

As Christians, we must reach out to understand. We must see depression as a disease, something that is treatable, but we also must not turn our heads and act as if people who suffer from depression are a disgrace or a failure. Mercy is the gift we were given by God. The compassion and grace given to each of us by Him in our weakest time of struggle is the gift we can give in Christ to each other.

Finish Second

~

When I lost my marriage, I made the ridiculous assumption that, somewhere out there on that cosmic scale where things are weighed in the kingdom of justice, it was time for my ship to come in. The law of averages alone seemed to point in my favor, as God only gives us what we can bear and I felt I had borne my fair share of losses. Any day now, the tide would turn for the better. It was time for God to "kick in." After all, didn't He owe me a break in the love department?

I shudder to think of how shallow my faith was and how raw my raw spots of recovery and healing were. God had patiently allowed me to suffer, be hurt, and fall flat over my pride and presumptions many times. After enough pain and embarrassment, the truth began to dawn on my heart that I deserved only death in this world, and that God had given me much to be grateful for in spite of the divorce and ensuing years of depression and failed relationships.

Marriage was not the end-all answer to my problem.

Each of us has our own Achilles' heel—that part of us which is most tender and vulnerable. Being a musical theater fan, I often think of Stephen Sondheim's song "Anyone Can Whistle," and how he wonders in this candid song about why simple things are hard for him. Why has finding a solid, godly relationship with a man been so hard for me? The singing and writing and "harder" endeavors come so naturally. But when it comes to my soul's underbelly—being in love—I can't seem to "whistle."

I grew up singing, doing theater and performing, sharing my feelings and communicating through song as an occupation. I have braved the terror of auditions for commercials and parts and have put myself in vulnerable situations with little thought about failing or succeeding. But the seemingly simple things like falling in love—that's where I've had great difficulty in judgment and discernment and in faith.

As a divorced, single-again woman, I still couldn't whistle. My heart goes out to the men I "learned on" through various dating experiences and relationships. And I hope that God used us to teach each other to draw closer to Him in our desires of the heart. But my frustrations increased as the years passed by, and God still seemed to turn a deaf ear to my prayers for a godly remarriage.

Finally, I began to see that my dreams for a second marriage had become an idol in my life. It took me a long time to realize that I had things out of order. My dreams had taken over my sanity at times, keeping me emotionally off balance. Then one summer, I knew it was time to "lay my Isaac" down. I had to die to my dream, give it to God, and trust that He would do the right thing for me and for my children.

At this point, the Lord began to woo me through a startling time of renewal. A good friend recommended that I do the *Experiencing God* study. And so I bought the book, and after getting Courtney and Graham off to school each day, sat down and dove into the study. Through this the Holy Spirit moved in and gently, sweetly cleansed and healed me. I believe this book is truly anointed, and I recommend it to everyone—especially to single parents and to people who feel they've lost hope or freshness in their walk with God.

Being broken down in heart and open to God, with nothing else standing between us, led me to be utterly dependent on Him for the first time in my life. And He met me with an intensity of love and intimacy I had never before known.

God began to impress upon me how much He loved me. He loved me with a jealous love. He was a protective husband, father, giver, and romancer—all at once! I started to taste how much God missed me. What a concept! He had been dealing with my pleading and praying for a husband, listening to me rant and rave about how lonely I was, when there He stood, able to satisfy me all along.

I spent more and more time reading the Word and just being still before Him. I would take a blanket and go to a nearby park and just be—just be with Him. Flooded with the presence of God, I heard Him say to me over and over, "Seek Me first, Bonnie. Seek Me first. Then it will be all right. However things go, trust Me, and come here first."

Then a great realization dawned on me: If I let God's arms hold me first, then the right man—His man—could hold me in time.

And the most amazing thing happened. My fears left me. The fears that I might never remarry, that my career might never recover, that my finances might always be in disarray—all these fears left me. I was no longer afraid of what life could do to me. I had prayed for deliverance, and it would come—however God orchestrated it. God answers prayers. And His answer, thus far, had been negative. Wonder of wonders, my eyes began to open to the beauty of the word "no." That word became my resting place.

I'd had it all backward. I'd been trying to settle for lesser relationships because I didn't think God would allow me to have what I truly wanted in a marriage. Oh, me of little faith! My prayers began to be redefined and refined by His presence. And my heart changed dramatically. Being grounded in a place of trusting God's refusals led me into a much-needed valley of peace. I felt a new desire awaken in me—a desire for a man who would long for this same place of peace. My prayers for remarriage did not end; they deepened and matured and relaxed into a prayer for a man who would always let me finish second—behind my Lord.

With ever-increasing power, God drew me closer and closer to Him. I didn't want anything ever to disrupt the beautiful love I had always longed for—and now finally was finding in His arms. But I would ask in Jesus' name for a godly man to come into my life. I would imagine what it would feel like to be in love with someone who loved God so much that his main concern would be not breaking God's heart above mine!

I was tired of being a fool when it came to love and tired of feeling like I was at the mercy of searching for love, not being able to whistle the right tune to find it. I learned to pray the prayer that Mary prayed when the angel told her she would deliver God's Son even though she was unmarried and a virgin: "Be it done unto me according to Thy will." These words became my own prayer that I would utter under my breath when paying bills, when frustrated in the grocery-store line, when worried and alone in the dark at night. I prayed these words as a response to the enemy's attempts to throw me off. I prayed these words as a blessing—that God was forever and always looking out for me in eternal ways that I might never understand but needed to believe were for my own good.

Our God is the God of the impossible. I believe that He honors dreams and prayers with His answers and in His time. So often in the Bible, God moved in seemingly hopeless situations to show His astounding love. And for anyone who is divorced—or otherwise hopeless—this condition offers ripe opportunity for God's mercy to become real.

The divorced, the depressed, the single, the single parents—these people abound in, live, walk, and survive in crisis. And I know firsthand how frustrating it is to go to school functions where everyone around you looks like a couple, and you feel like you have a big "D" branded on your forehead. It's hard to go to church and feel like a second-class citizen. It's hard to look around the carpool line and feel embarrassed and worried to the bone about taking your children home to a fatherless house. It's hard to work all day, running all over town, praying to make ends meet, praying that you'll be enough for everyone, dropping into bed each night afraid to pray—yet needing so very much to pray.

It all comes down to trust...and faith...and accepting God's answers—whatever they are. It all comes down to believing that God is the God of the impossible and that He yearns to love us "in the middle"—especially in the middle of crisis. These times in our lives are precious chances to believe in and discover Someone who loves us so much that He became like us, coming down here and diving into the crisis with us. These times are seasons for us to believe in miracles in the face of silence. And they are times to love God first and pray that those closest to us might love God enough to let us finish second to Him.

One
COLORS

Two
RED

Three
ORANGE

Four
YELLOW

Five
GREEN

Six
BLUE

Seven
PURPLE

Eight
RAINBOW

Faith means believing in advance, what will happen in reverse.

—Philip Yancey, *Where Is God When It Hurts?*

1996

This week, major revelation: There is nothing sexier, more appealing, more inviting as a quality in a man than godliness! That is THE ultimate! I am praying with earnest trust for a man who loves the Lord first, then me and my children. I want a guy who doesn't necessarily fit into the mold of this culture, but is God's person. No wonder I haven't married before now. The men were precious and dear, but neither of us put God first. It's starting to make sense to me now.

1996

It's never too late—because of Jesus.

April, 1997 (St. Catherine, Canada, Dove Awards night)

Tonight God reached out like a big, strong, gentle Father, full of patience, to reassure me that He hears my heart. One of the faculty members playing for the high school choir had been listening to me share about being a single mom at the afternoon question/answer session. He came up to me before the concert and shared with me about his second marriage of twelve years and God's faithfulness in his and his wife's lives. He said, "Wait...God is working." Those were his exact words. I had to try not to cry because I was overwhelmed with God's love that had reached out through this stranger to encourage me. I am staggered by these moments.

1997

The latest date was a terrible disaster. After the date is over, after the guy is gone...Oh well, wrong again. This guy is nothing like what I thought. He was a monster. Now I am filled with a mixture of feelings ranging from disappointment to anger to shame to rage and then exhaustion. Am I just absolutely clueless, beyond help when it comes to men?

1997

God knows the heart, and He knows that my intentions were good....He can use this, and I must fight the places in me that urge me to wallow in my bad judgment. The enemy is certainly coming after me with a string of Ishmaels—attempts to assault my faith because I am vulnerable in these issues of love and men. But I insist on waiting, hoping, and expecting in the name of I AM for peace, victory, and remarriage.

1997

I really am excited to see who God has for me. I believe there could be a most wonderful, godly man in my future. I feel like I'm being sanded and honed for this man. God has spared me from myself and from settling for less, and I daily pray that in His time, I will have His man in my life.

October, 1997

I've met my *story* and his name is Brent.

To Brent:

You're building a house on a farm under the stars that I long to share. I want to sit with you on the porch at night and talk about God and life, dreams and children and love. I want you to see my children grow up and out and on and to hold my hand to help me let them go. And when God allows the day to come, I want you to be there when Cheyenne comes to find you. I'm a little taller but when you hold me I am weak in the knees. You are strong and male and godly. You love horses and open skies and there is such mystery in your face. It's a mystery I want to be trusted with. I want to belong to you. I want you to love me.

April, 2000

I am happily remarried and building a new life now. I still wrestle with the injustices of life, but the desperate moments are further and further apart. The most precious assurance of all is that I know where to go when the desolation threatens even here on our lovely farm, with my Brent, with my children, with my work, and with my heart at peace. Having no clue how long this season of my life will be a sweet respite, I have to ask God to never let me forget what He's taught me in the dark. But I do know that nothing in life is predictable, and that can be the beauty of it. Because in the glory and the desperation, we have Christ, and so we cope and continue to hope.

Just One More

~

*Endurance is not just the ability
to bear a hard thing,
but to turn it into glory.*

—WILLIAM BARCLAY

The final process of writing a song called "My Beloved" that's been brewing in me for a long time has been a satisfying experience. It's a love song from God to man that speaks of the sacred romance that started in Eden and continues now through the drone and noise and confusion of the world like a steady symphony that refuses to be silenced.

Yet simultaneously, as the heavenly love song plays, there's another dissonant song, out of tune, which threatens to drown it out. The ugliness of the lyrics that sing of relentless tragedies never ceases to catch me off guard.

On a flight out of town this weekend, I heard of an acquaintance of mine whose nine-year-old daughter had just been killed in a senseless car accident. This mother is a godly, good woman who lives for the Lord and who is now suffering through the unthinkable process of giving her daughter back to God at such a young age. It's almost impossible to pray for such a situation without fear stopping me down. Fear that God really isn't in control. Fear that if I think about it too much, I could become so angry at God for standing by and continuing to watch the slaughter of innocents as if His hands were tied. Fear that I might just not ever be able to pray again. Or believe anymore in the love song I just penned.

As I pray a forced prayer for this friend who lost her daughter, I have this image of God, our Father, *the Father,* and I see Him in heaven weeping so loudly, with an other-world agony. This sound sends the angels to cover their tear-streaked faces in a place where I know tears are outlawed. I imagine when the unthinkable happens, God's cries ring with a deafening sound that defeats our own. I see Christ on the cross, looking out at us all and saying, "It is finished!" knowing that the unbearable will now be made bearable because of His holy, human blood.

And yes, I know that God, the life-giver, the Son-giver, doesn't miss a beat regarding the deaths, the illnesses, the births that go awry, the marriages that fail, the ones who are beaten down. It wasn't supposed to be this way. His church, His beloved—we are so loved that He came down and gave Himself away to prove it.

Free will ties the pierced hands in a way that I will never quite understand, a way that is hard to accept. But somehow in the process, I see the glimmer of a love that is so enormous that it asks us to try to grasp the notion that, for now, the drops of red that fell from Christ are still being used. Not one drop will be wasted.

It's almost like I hear the voice of God speaking to me, "It's not yet time...because I wait for all to come...there's just one more...then another...just one more...please know that I see and that I will judge and that all is not lost...but for now Love waits for that just one more."

So the symphony plays on through the cacophony, to arouse and to call the remaining precious ones with a love I cannot deny. If it were the death of *my* child lying in the balance, I wonder how I'd have a shred of that "amazing grace" left to see the need and to wait for that just one more. And then I am flooded again with my own unworthiness, knowing that these glasses we see in are still so terribly dark and clouded.

May God grant us all the ability to hear the song He sings when the world turns upside down and tastes bitter. May we hear His crying as it mixes with our own. May we know that Christ gladly bears the price of loss and pain with us, and that someday the crying will end forever when the real love song begins.

Something to
Hold On To

~

How easy it is to search for a "way" or a "truth" that might promise life apart from Jesus, in what I call the "almost enough" solutions offered by our culture.

The enemy loves to lure and tempt and offer "almost enough" to keep us on a path of subtle deception. In my estimation, there are many elements of biblical principle to be found in contemporary self-help—and even New Age—philosophies. But inherently in each of these viewpoints and offerings is the underlying message that we can fix ourselves through whatever that particular program offers. We can still be in control of our recovery.

For me, this theory stops just short of the real deal. Jesus seems to be missing or, at best, diffused in terminology. "Higher powers" are a start. But His name must be the end. Any precept that bases itself on anything other than the cross of Jesus is ultimately doomed. It's such old hat to Satan—this lie he continues to offer, repackaged and upgraded, but the same old song and dance. You can be your own god. You can determine your own destiny. You can empower yourself with the right tools to overcome anything and discover your worth and potential. You can be part of the universe and connected to all living energy. The drug of pride keeps working, and mankind continues to follow after anything that will keep self-reliance intact. How frightening and how very un-American it is to fall facedown in worship before an almighty, sovereign God.

Mother Teresa's death was a huge loss to our world. I can think of no one anywhere in my lifetime who lived such a clearly selfless life for Jesus. And her death also offered a challenge for us all—especially for the media. What would they do with the name of Jesus, which this amazing woman blatantly invoked as the sole source for her inspiration and from which she gathered the strength and faith to touch more hurting people than anyone else in modern history?

To say the word "God" is fairly acceptable in our culture. Athletes, actors, just about anyone onstage or in the limelight for any achievement will throw out his or her acknowledgment of God. But the name of Jesus just kind of sticks out there, doesn't it? It's just too archaic, too right-wing, too...uncomfortable. Jesus the Christ is not politically correct.

After Mother Teresa died, one media outlet asked, "Now that Mother Teresa is gone, who do we look to?"

"How about God?" someone dared to suggest.

How about Jesus?

Marty and I recently sang at a wonderful church where the pastor had asked a congregation member who owned a farm to cut down the largest tree he could find and to make a rough-hewn cross from this tree. When we arrived to do sound check on that Sunday morning, we literally gasped at the sight of this huge cross sitting dead center in the middle of the platform. It was so large and so in-the-way that we either had to walk around it or out from behind it to sing or to speak. The message was unmistakable.

There stands a cross that must be dealt with. There is no program that prepares one for this challenge, and none is needed. It is there—unavoidable and completed. This cross is such a problem for so many. It is uniquely alone among world religions—our Father God, through the incarnation of His Son, hangs bloodied in a passionate display of love unthinkable and scandalous.

By not making himself exempt, but by delib-
erately taking on the worst the world has to
offer, Jesus gave us the hope that God can
likewise transform the suffering each of us
must face. Because of his death and resurrection, we can confidently assume that no
trial—illness, divorce, unemployment, bank-
ruptcy, grief—extends beyond the range of
his transforming power.

—PHILIP YANCEY, *Where Is God When It Hurts?*

In a world that offers many solutions and programs and
drug therapies and possibilities for healing the wounded
heart and soul, I offer the cross of Christ. Take it or leave it.
But if you do have the courage to take it, take it with you
along any of the other paths you may be led to explore. It
will go with you. Take this cross with you, hold it close,
embrace it for yourself with a simple openness, and it will
hold you up. In the meantime, dare to discover this man
named Jesus, eternal God wrapped in human skin, who
transforms you through His cross into someone who will not
only survive but will also overcome the pain of divorce.

At the onset of my divorce, I desperately wanted to find
something to hold on to. It took me awhile, but God patiently
allowed me to discover what was in front of me all the time.
The cross and only the cross cuts deep across every line in
my heart and beyond every pain and loss that divorce has
brought into my life and into the lives of my children. And
ultimately, nothing but the cross of Christ will move me on.

The single most effective medicine I have found as a
divorced, single parent—and woman—is studying how Jesus
dealt with women. To reprogram my own self-esteem
through the eyes of the One who made me has been a rebirth
of unspeakable joy. I'm finding the child/teenager/former
wife/young mother/divorced dreamer pieces of myself that
cry out to be defined through the words of Christ. I am

learning to ask His opinion about these vulnerable places in my soul, and as I read about His encounters with women of His day, I see grace and mercy and overwhelming love.

Go back and dive into the story of the woman at the well—a Samaritan who, in that day and time, had the double-whammy stigma of being both a woman and an inhabitant of the lowest-rent part of the region. Look at how Jesus *knew* how many times she had failed. Yet behold His grace and scandalous compassion.

Jesus was the most real human being who ever lived. He cut right through to the heart of where a person was and then poured healing into the deepest wound. One of the best examples of how we "failures" are loved by our God can be seen in the example of how even the rowdy lady Rahab, a prostitute, ends up in the Hebrews 11 hall of fame. God looked past her sin to her heart of faith. I also love the story of the adulteress who Jesus advised to "go and sin no more." The Word *doesn't* tell us that Jesus then went into the village to which she had to return and fixed her circumstances. All of us must walk out the consequences of our choices. But oh, the grace that abounds in that journey is the miracle of what we believe and what He gives.

Jesus was tender and precious to all women, and not just to the good little faithful synagogue-attenders. He went out to touch the big-time losers, the ones who had little to hold on to, the ones who needed a man to reach out and validate and love them right where they were.

In spite of the tatters and tears that make up the life of a woman after divorce—plagued with doubts about her own worth and what little pieces of hope she has for the future— I would say, whatever it takes you to get there, you must, must, must make your way to the arms of Christ. Nothing else comes close to the healing that waits for you there.

Trust God
and Enjoy the Kiwi

~

At the end of the day, at the end of this book, how do things stand in my life? I didn't realize until recently how this book would end. My focus has been on sharing the struggles of being a divorced single parent in our culture from a perspective of having lived it and breathed it. I know that depression will mostly likely be a cross for me to bear until I see the Lord. When I had first finished writing this book, no husband was waiting in the wings, but I had great peace in God's sufficiency. I believed I had pegged my calling. I was to minister to singles as a single—forever if God willed it—and I was to minister with joy. Okay. Got it. And my prayers for love and remarriage were allowed to continue. With perspective and balance, I could share that also. Terrific.

About this time, when I had everything all figured out and the third or fourth draft of this book crept through my Macintosh printer, God surprised me with the answer to my seven-year prayer. Suddenly and swiftly, in a fashion that only God could orchestrate, a wonderful friend of mine—a friend I had known 20 years—and I began to see each other. We fell madly in love. We did things right. We waited on God's leading, and we were married. God has answered my prayers for a second chance at love and marriage. And this doesn't fit in the book anywhere! I experienced a strange sense of guilt when I realized I had been removed from the demographic I so deeply came to feel—and still do feel—empathy and kinship for.

I believe now that the Lord wanted me to complete this writing with only His arms around me. Actually, that has been my greatest joy in the process—being able to write from a hopeful heart with no visible signs of the end of my rainbow. And I know from personal experience that this new marriage is not the answer to the empty space in my heart that still only my Father God can fill.

God may or may not move each of us into remarriage. That's not the key to our peace, nor to our conquering the demons that divorce and depression leave with us. It is my utter conviction that there is holiness in each day, in each place God has us, in each moment, if we look for it. We need to see God as our ally, the friend of our right hand, and not the indifferent, distant dictator who takes no real interest in every little wisp of wind that we breathe. Jesus is the Word, the only truth and life we have, and we must do as Frederick Buechner suggests and allow Him to be a "tiger in our blood."

First Call sang for a singles' event in Vancouver, British Columbia, a few years ago, where one of the pastors shared a story I will never forget. This pastor had worked extremely hard for many weeks and had an upcoming business trip that would take him to a province in the middle regions of Canada for a few days. He was looking forward to the trip even though it was business-related. He knew he'd have the silence of the long airplane ride and a few days away from the hubbub of his daily responsibilities.

Finally the day of departure arrived. He went to the airport in great spirits, upgraded his ticket to business class as a special treat, and buckled in for the journey. This pastor was one of those people who love flying, so he had little anxiety about anything going wrong. He was doubly thrilled to see the menu the flight attendant handed him, which showed that he would get a fabulous meal, starting out with an appetizer which included his favorite fruit—kiwi. The plane took off and everything was going great—for a while—at least long enough for the flight attendants to serve the people in business class the first course of their meal—the kiwi. Then out of nowhere, the plane began to nosedive. The captain's voice came on and told the attendants to sit down immediately and asked for everyone to stay calm. Of course everyone went bonkers. People were yelling and food was flying and panic was everywhere. The pastor looked around and decided right then and there, "I know who I am and where I'm going. If this plane goes down, it goes down. But I've waited a long time for this, so I'm just going to trust God and enjoy the kiwi." Which is exactly what he did. He grabbed ahold of his tray and that gorgeous green fruit and savored every bite, while all around him the world seemed to be going down for the last time. (Now obviously, the plane leveled off and everything ended happily, or the pastor wouldn't have been around to share this profound analogy.)

When I heard his story, I was tremendously moved by his faith and optimism. I decided this would be a wonderful statement by which to live: "Trust God and enjoy the kiwi." Life is what it is, but Jesus overcame this world. Divorce, depression, loss, betrayal, hurt, and pain are part of the nosedives that come and go for all of us. But there is a mystery in the nosedive, if we can find it. Holiness is all around us in the blessings of our friends, our families, our children, our work, and this precious, good earth God has given us to walk on for a brief time. My prayer for any of us who feel that the weight of the day is too heavy, the cross too costly, the picture too disappointing, is that we can remember the rainbow—God's promise to be faithful for us. Let us learn to lean on the character of God and not to miss this life or be robbed of its beauty. May we live holding on to Christ alone, and through His Holy Spirit be given the grace to trust God and enjoy the kiwi!

Baptism

~

Never say never.

If someone had told me that my children would be baptized in the same baptistery I was, at the same church I was raised in, I would have quietly smiled at the absurdity of the thought. If someone had told me that at the ceremony I would stand side by side with my children's father, his mother, my mother, and my new husband, I would have started to snicker. If someone had told me that my daughter and son would dutifully put on the white underwear, white gowns, and goofy caps the church kept in the dressing room for baptisms and then go into the freezing water where my father waited in a rubber suit to perform the ceremony, I would have belly-laughed.

Life, however, is never predictable.

My parents, Gwen and Fred, helped me raise my children. Before my divorce, they were loving and precious to us all. They loved Daniel and believed our marriage was perfect—which, by the way, is an impossible thing for any marriage to be. After the divorce, they continued to love Daniel with *agape* love and to honor him every time they interacted with him.

But as for me, my parents saved my life. They brought me into this world in 1955, and they gave me life again in 1990 when I was all but dead. Dad would come to my house to fix the washing machine or the garbage disposal, which I would inevitably break again by leaving something like a baby spoon in it. He moved furniture into and out of my home, and he never questioned me. We began a relationship we'd never had when I was a child. I became daddy's needy little girl when I was in my mid-thirties.

My mom, God bless her, brought the same energy she'd poured out on my siblings and me when we were children to my situation as an adult. She rose to every task, helping to raise another set of kids—her grandchildren—when she and dad deserved to be taking trips to Europe and enjoying lazy afternoons at home. They drove carpool to ball games and play rehearsals and cooked and cleaned and moved things and paid for clothes, shoes, and school tuition.

I cannot say enough about how much I love and honor my parents. Without them, I could not have survived.

And so when it came time for my children to be baptized, we had a lot of questions about how and when and who would do the honors. My father had been an elder in the church, and I could think of no one more precious and dear to baptize my children than my daddy. He was very moved when I asked him, and it seemed like a gift I could give both him and my children.

Of course, before the music swells and this image transcends into a movie moment, let me tell you something. On the day that we all planned to converge on the church building, no one had turned on the heater in the baptistery. The water was absolutely, screaming cold.

Mom freaked. Dad was calm. I freaked. The kids were calm.

Their father Daniel arrived with his mom. My great-aunt Helen's daughter was in town, and so I invited her to the event. However, she had to stand guard by the door to let in my husband Brent, who was rushing to the church from a session he was producing.

Courtney looked at the huge white undies and gown and shower cap and tried to be kind. I looked at her and started laughing. "Just put it on," I said.

Graham and his dad went into the men's changing room to find a gown small enough to fit him.

Brent arrived. We were on.

I warned the kids that the water was freezing. Their eyes were huge. Mom panicked again, and I laughed.

Dad put on his rubber overalls and got into the water, ready for whoever was brave enough to come join him.

I stood side by side with my children's father and new stepfather and both grandmothers and a precious cousin and my dad, who said the sweetest words in the world over my babes: "I now baptize you in the name of the Father, Son, and the Holy Spirit."

Both kids were silent and blue-lipped and shivering as they went into the icy water. Courtney let out an "Ahh!" but never stopped walking. Graham looked at me and cringed, but made his way to my dad.

Daniel prayed for them. I read them a letter I had written to them and gave each of them a copy of it.

Then we left. We walked out into the night air and drove away in separate cars to return to our separate lives. The air seemed cold, but somehow warmer because of the event that had just taken place—this impossible, never-say-never event that happened because of a cross, where the Son of God makes all things possible.

Blessed Are the Desperate

~

Every time I sing, I meet people who tell me they are at the end of their rope. They tell me they identify with my songs of pain and hope all mixed together. It's the hope they want to feel and believe. They want the peace that Jesus promises, but they often feel stuck in the dark places of fear, sadness, or simply loneliness.

It's in the loneliness that we connect.

"How did you ever get to that place of peace?" they ask, recognizing that their pain has been mine.

I tell them how 12 years of everything that seemed sacred to me seemed to crash and burn all at once—my ten-year marriage, my life's work of music ministry, my sense of self and confidence in my ability to mother, and even my rational mind as I spiraled downward into clinical depression.

Single again at age 35, with two small children, I felt lost in a dark fog as to who I was as a woman and a Christian. Suddenly in this demographic that I did not choose—Divorced White Female of Faith—I woke every morning only to struggle through another agonizing day of trying to make sense of the stress, finances, hormones, and fragments of failed relationships.

The music I'd been making all my life as a backup singer on the road and in studios for friends like Amy Grant, Sandi Patty, and Russ Taff—as well as in my own Christian music group, First Call—suddenly sounded strange.

I too asked, "Was this what Jesus died for, a life marked by failure, depression, and hanging on by my fingernails?" I too felt like maybe my choice to believe in the peace of Christ was a sham. *How can I live out what my songs insist,* I wondered— *that God does deliver us from even ourselves?*

In those dark moments, usually late in the night when I lay alone in bed, reworking all my mistakes, searching for ways to fix or find purpose in all the personal failures, the music quieted. Desperate in the silence, I thought of the hope God has promised, hope of a more abundant life, not just in heaven, but right here, right now.

Is this the way You designed life to be? I'd pray. *Will my faith make it through this in one piece? Who will I be on the other side—and is there an "other side"?*

As I thought more of Him and less of me, I began to hear a voice calling from beyond my circumstances. I recognized a familiar timbre of pain as the voice spoke about similar betrayals, despair, and heartbreak in relationships and life's work.

And I thought of the questions Jesus asked. I wondered about those hours He'd hung on the cross. I imagined the doubts the demons must have whispered into His ears. Somehow Christ knew that by embracing His own death, life would be born. So I learned to try to listen for God to speak to me through my own hours of desperation. "Please…some relief," I'd pray, "…anything that shows progress…let my heart be made new."

Often I heard only tears, sometimes silence, and then finally this: Every crash site can be holy ground. Nothing is wasted. Every moment matters.

Love brought Jesus to His crash site so that my search for love wouldn't leave me hurting on my own. Only that love can sustain me when life throws the one-two punch and I'm down for the count. Only that love remained when my marriage and music died and my work, ministry, and pride died with it. When all that was left for me was the sacrificial love of God, His Son, and His Spirit, my true peace began.

My desolation, my crash site, was my salvation—because it was there that I finally broke apart and let in the mercy of Christ. As Jesus spoke to me about the meek, the lowly, the poor in spirit, at last I came to understand the mystery of undeserved favor and to see how weakness indeed can be used for great mercy.

Blessed are the desperate.

One
COLORS

Two
RED

Three
ORANGE

Four
YELLOW

Five
GREEN

Six
BLUE

Seven
PURPLE

Eight
RAINBOW

Your love changes every-
thing
Dark to perfect dawn
A beacon of reasoning in
a sky that leads me on
Let lesser dreams fade
from view
Mine will begin and end
with you
Your love changes every-
thing

—Bonnie Keen, Scott Brasher, and Michael
Standifer, from "Your Love Changes Everything"

Holy Ground

~

Before I describe the picture of my life on the other side of desperation, I must state emphatically that the peace I found with God came in the middle of darkness. When I stopped trying to create my own definition of peace, my eyes were at last opened to a beautiful vista I had previously been blind to. And the wooing of the Lord brought me to rest in His vision for my life, to try to live accepting the grace of Christ.

As I finished the writing of songs for *Marked for Life* and continued to write and rewrite this book, I thought, "Now I get it! My mission in life is to embrace wherever God has me, and for now that's single and broke, and healing and finding happiness in life's adventure, in every twist and turn."

The contentment that has been a balm to my soul did not come from a man. It was the mercy of Jesus that finally filled me up so that I was not afraid of losing out or missing out or of being a failure. At last I was at home in my own skin, in my own basket-case kind of humanity. Remarriage was not the big bingo prize. It was, in fact, a total surprise.

By the time I met Brent, I'd been through so many near misses, broken engagements, and messy breakups that my daughter looked at me and begged, "Please, Mom, don't date anymore. You'll just get engaged again!" I assured her that Brent and I were great friends and that was all there was to it. Of course, by the end of our first date, we both knew that we were falling in love.

Interesting thing about God. He has a surprising, hilarious, sense of humor. Look at what He did in the Bible—giving 96-year-old Sarah a baby shower, having donkeys speak wisdom. Or when it came time for Him to come to us, having His Son born in a hick town called Bethlehem to a couple of teenagers. His eleventh-hour rescues drive me batty. You never know what God has up His sleeve.

So, having convinced myself that there were no more good men left in the world, God allowed *two* awesome men to come into my life. They were complete opposites, but both absolute jewels. I imagined God smiling, arms folded, and saying, "So, Miss Know-It-All, you thought there were no good men left! Well, here are two of My best. You now have a choice of who you will give your heart to."

And once again, had I not waited for God's man—for His plan and timing—I would have missed out on Brent, the man whom I love and adore in a way I'd been begging God to allow me to experience.

Brent and I first met when we were in our early twenties, before either of us had been married. At the time I was engaged to my first husband. (When he was ten, Graham called me "the engagement magnet," and after further observation of my breakups, observed, "Mom, you're a dumping kind of gal!") Brent was a brilliant young recording engineer, already working with country artists such as Reba McEntire and making a name for himself in the industry. I was singing and dancing and acting in commercials and trying to find where I would land artistically. We wouldn't date until 20 years later, after I'd been divorced for many years, and after he had just gone through his own devastating divorce and loss of the son he thought was his own.

Brent was the recording engineer on many sessions I was hired to sing on over the years, and the community of singers, producers, writers, and artists in Nashville is relatively small and tight. So we were all shocked and hurting for Brent as we watched him go on with his life. He looked like he'd been through hell. He'd lost a lot of weight and seemed like a man whose guts had been wrenched out. Yet the way he moved ahead with his work and life and still kept his sense of humor intact never ceased to amaze me. My pastor was one of the great men who held on to Brent during this time, at times calling him at midnight to see how he was doing. I had always admired Brent, but watching him deal with his pain so humbly and honestly made him even more special in my eyes. I journaled about him and asked God to bring him a young wife who could give him ten kids to make up for the loss of his son. Little did I know that I was praying myself into his life.

I'd begun to communicate and meet with another incredible, attractive, godly man who was a professor at a college I'd visited. I knew that this man was someone special and that we were on the road to getting serious, but I still had this nagging thing about Brent in the back of my mind. So I got down on my knees early one morning and prayed, "God, if there's something I need to know about Brent, will You please let me know soon? This is driving me nuts!"

That afternoon, Brent called.

On our first date, he smiled at me and said, "I remember what you were wearing the first time I saw you in 1971." (Now, that's a line you don't hear every day!) Then he clearly described the exact attire, down to the boots, that I was wearing when I had sung at his college that fall. Well, what's a girl to do with that? He had me—hook, line, and sinker.

We were married in the carriage house of a Civil War mansion in January of 1998. It was a small ceremony/celebration that we shared with all of the people who have known both of us for twenty years—the people who have prayed with us, cried with us, listened to us, and hoped for answers with us. Brent and I were there when the guests arrived, and we wandered around talking to people until the actual ceremony began. Then everyone gathered around us and my children, and our pastor, Scotty Smith, did a free-form kind of rap through the vows, rocking back and forth on his heels, loving so much seeing the fruit of our pain redeemed. He knew both of our histories so well, and he knew exactly what from us would speak most powerfully to each other. People cheered and clapped and shouted at times, and we cried and laughed. It was a rowdy, glorious night. I'd had a chance to pray over the room by myself earlier that week. I wanted the Spirit of God to be all over everything—from the cake and food and flowers to the hearts and tenor of the ceremony. It was, as I said in our wedding invitation, "To our God who is exceedingly able to do more than we can ask or imagine..." a blessed event.

Then of course, we dove into the reality of blending our lives together. Brent, Courtney, Graham, and I were eating dinner together one night early on, and Graham said this prayer that I think pretty much says it all: "God, thank You for this new time in our lives...and...uh...God, just show us how to do this!"

Courtney was fourteen and Graham was ten when I remarried. Brent calls Courtney "Queen" and melts every time she enters a room, something she is learning to take full advantage of. Graham is being immersed in a man's world more than ever as Brent teaches him to ride horses and to fish in our pond. Yes, we moved to a farm, and I feel a little like Lisa in "Green Acres." I'm usually fine—unless I see some kind of small critter a little too close to the house. And last fall we had an entire family of deer in our driveway!

But things aren't all easy or perfect now. We have a family counselor who we go to and talk with from time to time, as there are many new hurdles and challenges that have come with the marriage. But not a day goes by that I do not thank God for His grace in bringing Brent into my life and into my children's lives. He is a brave soul, my Brent, taking on me and my wildly creative and spirited children. My nickname is "Lucy" because of the myriad of strange little accidents that seem to surround me (like the time I was driving Brent's car to the bank and hit the pole by the drive-up window). I thank God that he can laugh at the series of "adjustment" episodes that have accompanied our first years together.

Presently I am touring and speaking, learning as I go how to drop the veil from my life in the most effective way to help speak hope to others. Brent engineered and produced my new recording project, which was another healing experience for us, and he accompanied me on the road for my first solo concert. On the road, I am overwhelmed by how the project—just pieces of my life revealed as honestly as I can reveal them—opens the doors for others to realize their own pain and their need for God's touch. After my first concert, in which I spoke of the near–date rape experience I'd had, the first three women in line to talk with me confessed that they had been date-raped. One even had had a child from that harrowing episode. "No one ever talks about anything like this...thank you," I kept hearing. One woman fell on me before I could get to the back of the auditorium, just weeping and weeping. Another lady—at a mall appearance, of all places—grabbed me, tears streaming down her face. She couldn't even tell me how to pray for her. She just said, "Thank you...I can't talk about it," and left.

All I know is that God is allowing me this time and season to be as vulnerable as I can about my past and to speak hope about what He alone has done to redeem and bless my life. Brent is the miracle in my life—the man I prayed my children might know, the man I can love. But miracles come in all sorts of ways, and the winds of grace blow a steady stream of mercy throughout all of our lives.

I'm enjoying this time of knowing that each day is holy ground, grateful for the chance to invite others to step out—in Christ's name and time and purpose and plan—and find the holy ground that waits for them. I thank God that He allowed me to hurt deeply enough to give me a heart of compassion for others who go through the Valley of Baca, that place of tears. And I pray that He will never let me forget, not even for a moment, what it feels like to be under the water and fighting for air.

Precious to me, in a special way, are the most desperate and broken of us. I pray that the waters of redemption and healing will drench our hearts with all He died to bring us—true life.

Epilogue

~

Scotty Smith

The Scriptures teach us to encourage one another and all the more as we see the Day of Christ approaching (Hebrews 10:25). Walking with Bonnie over the last several years as her pastor, brother in Christ, and friend has been just such an encouragement to my own needy heart. But this is an afterword, not a eulogy to be read at her funeral! Bonnie is not the point—the God of all grace is. It is with pleasure that I hold out some of the many things that Bonnie did well in the strength of that grace as encouragement to all who have read her story.

Galatians 6:9 invites us to "not become tired of doing good. We will receive our harvest...at the right time if we do not give up." Bonnie sowed her tears and is reaping the first fruits of joy in the morning because. . .

1. She continued to take her argument to God. Literally for years Bonnie and I met in my office and she tenaciously made God the issue in her drama. "Scotty, where is God in this?" she would passionately ask. Like Job she refused to settle for easy answers, biblical Band-Aids, or crutches. Bonnie persisted in wrestling with the angel of the Lord.

2. She showed me an honest and painful willingness to take responsibility when, like Abraham, she was tempted to settle for Ishmael when God had promised Isaac. When Bonnie made unwise choices in her weariness she never pretended with me or made excuses. She repented and received grace.

3. Bonnie refused to allow shame and bitterness to take root and define her when her cry increasingly became "How long, O Lord?" (which by the way is the most-asked question in the Bible). I am amazed at how gentle she remained considering everything she went through. God can have such an effect in a hurting heart.

4. Her commitment to continually journal her fears, feelings, faith, and foibles kept Bonnie sane. I mean that. I am glad that her writings and wrangling are now showing up in print. To read the book of Psalms is to understand how healthy, freeing, and focusing it was (and is) for Bonnie to write out her internal struggle and give expression to the longings God placed within each of us.

5. Lastly, Bonnie's ongoing commitment to care for others in her great brokenness was powerful and convicting to me personally. When tempted to retreat into a black hole of victimization, she continued to move towards others. When joining the endless cycle of pity parties looked terribly inviting, Bonnie kept on singing the sufficiency of God's grace, loving her children, and being a good friend to so many of us.

As a living epistle, Bonnie invites all of us to keep on drinking from the river of grace, to collapse on Christ, and to trust boldly in the God of resurrection. Thank you, my precious sister, for making the gospel so attractive and believable!

My Hall of Famers

~

There is no way I would have survived and grown through my desperate years without God's best people, who I call my Hall of Famers. These women and men have graduate degrees in humanity—they know how to love and give and listen and really bear the burdens of the people they commit to.

Without my family, mom and dad, Stan and Amy, and then my second families—the Taffs, the Goldmans, the Mitchells, the Kleins, and the teachers and staff at CPA—my children and I would have never tasted the sweetness of real grace. The songs I was able to write during my weakest moments were really the doing of great writer friends like Lowell Alexander, Cheryl Rogers, Tori, Darrell, David, Kevin, Scott, and also came from the belief that Randy Cox and Donna Hilley gave me at Sony ATV Publishing. My basket-case traumas were lessened by the love of the women who made being 40 and single bearable: Nan, Carlana, Bev, Merrill Ann, Roberta, Vickie, Melodie, Cheryl, and Nanette. Over the years I've been the recipient of God's mercy through the literal hands-on rescue financially, spiritually, and emotionally of my precious mentors Nancy Alcorn and Dale Hanson Bourke.

Over the years I've also had men in my life who have been great safe places for me. On the road and in the studio, men like Marty McCall—brother of my heart and work—Max Lucado, Neal Joseph, Malcolm Greenwood, Dan Posthuma, David Arnholter, Steve Green, Wayne Watson, Mark Harris, Carman, Michael Omartian, Terry Choate, and many others have been there to pray with me, listen to me, and treat me with great respect and compassion. Many times I was graced by compliments of simple appreciation by these men who must have sensed my vulnerability and need for a pat on my fragile, woman's self-esteem.

Scotty Smith pastored me with elegant honesty and a pocket full of never-ending grace that helped me believe I could be forgiven for my past and could pray for a future while holding on to my dreams.

David McMillan was there for the dirt-flying ugliest chapters of my life and again was straight on with me in his counsel, in a way I treasure as persistent, much-needed tough love.

But in particular, I would never have learned the great perks of being a woman without being blessed by the best friend God ever gave a person—Tori Taff. She has been and continues to be the "sister I was separated from at birth." Not only is she one of the greatest lyricists and writers I know, but she can take over a roomful of people with her humor. She taught me to laugh in the pain, and just insisted I learn the fine art of treating myself to girly stuff—bubble baths and candles and days of doing pretty much nothing at all. This was unknown terrain for me, and her creative nurturing spirit inspired me to try to someday grow up to be her! Tori was always around night or day to pick up the phone and talk me through the wasteland years, even after the birth of her daughters. I have the coolest picture of her sitting right behind me at my second wedding, her beautiful, blonde head thrown back, laughing out loud and clapping as Brent and I kissed upon the pronouncement that we were "man and wife." Her husband, Russ, allowed me to be his sister and his backup singer and someone he would pray for and hook up television sets for and bring food to and even drive to the bus when a tour left in the freezing ice...just because he had a Jeep. They would never want it given much attention, but I know how wide the door is they've always left open for me.

Also, I am so very grateful for Roberta at CCM and for Terry and Carolyn and Janna at Harvest House Publishers, and for the staff at both Spring Hill Music Group and CCM for their courage in allowing me to spill my guts in song and on paper in the hope that it will touch a nerve somewhere out there to let other desperate ones know they are not alone. I thank Jeanette Thomason for her input and consultation on this book.

I thank God for all of my Hall of Famers. I really don't know how I can ever thank them. This side of paradise, they may never know how much I love them.